o.p. CD
650

D1301725

THE AMOROUS MASTER PEPYS

By the same Author:

LADIES OF THE HAREM

*By courtesy of the National Portrait Galle

SAMUEL PEPYS

THE AMOROUS
MASTER PEPYS

by

JAMES CLEUGH

FREDERICK MULLER LIMITED

LONDON

FIRST PUBLISHED BY FREDERICK MULLER LTD.
IN 1958
PRINTED AND BOUND IN GREAT BRITAIN BY
THE GARDEN CITY PRESS LIMITED
LETCHWORTH, HERTFORDSHIRE

COPYRIGHT © 1958 BY JAMES CLEUGH

Contents

Prologue

IT was on 1st January 1660, the year in which England was to have a king again after nearly a decade of dictatorship by a successful soldier, that Samuel Pepys, an obscure clerk in the office of Mr. George Downing, one of the four Tellers of the Receipt of Exchequer in London, sat down to keep a diary. He wrote it in cipher, for his own eye alone. He did not want anyone else to read it because he meant to put down everything he saw, heard, felt, thought or imagined, including certain scenes, words, emotions, ideas and fancies which hardly one of his contemporaries, even in that exceedingly frank age, would have dreamed of passing on, if only to an intimate friend. So he used a system of shorthand, which had been published by one Shelton in 1641. Moreover, he interlarded it, as time went on, with a good many words in French, Spanish and Latin, and even once or twice in Greek and Dutch, deliberately obscuring the sense so as to render it unintelligible to others—though his mis-spellings are probably inadvertent. But this hope of Samuel's, as we shall see, was by no means always fulfilled.

He was a round-faced young man of twenty-seven, stocky in build, sceptical, cautious and ambitious by temperament. He carried his five feet six inches with a strutting dignity when he walked, though the fine clothes which he loved were nearly always badly adjusted. In his work he was orderly and very industrious. But his native caution was always at odds with an unruly and impulsive emotional character, and this inner conflict emerged, among other less innocent manifestations of it, in the way he dressed.

It also appeared in his features. The long, fleshy nose stood for severity and application, but the eyes were restless and fervid, slightly suggesting those of a beast of prey. Inordinate use of his eyes both at work and at play was to weaken them desperately before long. They were eyes of the sort which are never still when they are open. So on sober occasions Mr. Pepys generally kept them half closed, which gave him the vigilant, quietly supercilious air that suits so well a conscientious Government official. It was contradicted, however, by the exce̶p̶t̶ ̶ ̶ ̶ ̶ ̶ ̶ ̶ ̶ ̶ ̶ ̶ ̶ ̶ ̶ ̶t̶h̶o̶s̶e̶ ̶ ̶o̶f̶ ̶a̶n̶ incorrigible sensu̶a̶ ̶

Mr̶.̶ ̶P̶e̶p̶y̶s̶ ̶not easy to read. It might have meant t̶h̶a̶t̶ ̶ ̶ ̶ ̶ ̶ ̶ ̶ ̶ ̶ ̶rchant or politician, greedy and ruthless, fond of women a̶n̶d̶ g̶o̶o̶d̶ living, a born dissembler. So he was, though not to any very dangerous extent. He disliked danger. No one was ever less of a man of action at heart, though could rise to play the part at times, as he did during the Dutch War and Great Fire of 1666. Samuel, however, was far more than a mere business man and intriguer with a perpetual itch for the company of good-looking girls. So commonplace a character, a mere precocious 'sugar-daddy', could not have survived to enthral those who live three hundred years after him.

The outstanding quality in Samuel Pepys was his wholly unconscious charm. It was innate, irresistible and owed nothing to culture or manners, in which he was somewhat deficient. He was not a wit, though he could be the life and soul of a party. He was not shy, though he was apt to be intimidated by his social superiors. Neither was he either noticeably senti-mental, high-spirited or eloquent. Certainly he was not physically radiant. He was not even particularly considerate of other peoples' feelings. He was just charming. Exactly what the nature of his charm was can only be discovered from read-ing his Diary, but it will be evident from the most casual glance at those immortal pages. Consequently, since the present sketch is not a psychological treatise, no further attempt need be made to define this in fact indefinable luggage that Pepys carried about with him.

He himself had not the faintest inkling of its existence. He was vain of other things, of his nose, of his old family, of his skill in music and his capacity for absorbing information, but not of what made, makes and will make so many different sorts of people love him. And yet it was an intense curiosity about himself, not unusual in men under thirty, which had caused Samuel to resolve to keep a journal. He had a naturally enquiring mind, which he felt it was easiest to exercise upon his own person and his reactions to the world about him.

That world, as he rightly perceived, was an exceptionally interesting one. The last half of the seventeenth century in England initiated in several important respects that in which we live today. Yet in others it looked back to mediæval times, as in the outward splendour and ceremony of its aristocratic society and the boisterous squalor of its far larger impoverished classes. Titled persons still lived feudally, but their ranks were being constantly extended by shrewd and industrious people like Samuel himself, who had no title at all. Men of even humbler birth than his, especially sailors like Sir William Batten and Admiral Lawson, reached high positions in his lifetime.

It was an age, as the foundation then of the Royal Society alone proves, of a wholly new scientific outlook, which Samuel Pepys shared. The superstitious inhibitions of the 'Gothic' centuries had to a great extent decayed, but formal religious observances and controversies still flourished. Samuel stood, so far as a plain man could, at the very centre of this somewhat contradictory state of affairs. He despised the fanatics who had survived from Cromwell's time; he laughed at the rising sect of Quakers who were to become so influential in the next century; but he went to church every Sunday, and occasionally he plopped down on his knees at home to pray to be delivered from his lusts.

He keenly criticised the style, if not the hackneyed content, of sermons. He did not care how long a good one lasted, for he could genuinely enjoy its technical elegance. But he was not really interested in religion for its own sake. In his philosophical moods, which never went very deep, he preferred to investigate the principles of mechanical or physiological marvels without trying to account for them theologically or metaphysically.

The world of Samuel Pepys had two other aspects, both founded in history and geography, which he found highly congenial. The naval feats of the last few reigns, especially under Elizabeth and Cromwell, had already established the characteristic sea power of his native island, by this date well on the way which it was to follow towards global empire during the next two hundred years. Pepys, in common with most of his fellow-countrymen of all classes at that time, was very proud of this achievement and was determined to maintain it. Nothing is more striking than the way in which the disgracefully treated ordinary seamen of the 1660s stuck to their work and their guns, in spite of frequent mutinous riots, at the most desperate crises of the Dutch wars. To patriots like Pepys England meant primarily ships and sailors—not statesmen and soldiers, still less the land itself and its institutions.

In the second place, the reaction of the Restoration period against Cromwellian austerity inaugurated, as everyone knows, more cynically unbridled sexual licence than had ever been known in the country before. It was not only that the turbulent and energetic islanders were largely in revolt against the imperative of mediæval Christianity to mortify the flesh in this world on pain of having it forcibly mortified by the hordes of Satan in the next; it was also the case that the insularity of English society remained for the time being less affected than the mainland of Europe by the ferment of rival but uniformly repressive moral systems, as in Holland and Spain especially, but also in the France of Louis XIV. Thus the swing of the pendulum in England, though historically motivated, was accelerated by the relative remoteness of the community from the centres of Western intellectual development.

Samuel happened to be a natural amorist, born into an environment exceptionally favourable to the exercise of erotic prowess. His performances in this direction are, however, more interesting than the commonplace debaucheries of the Buckinghams and Sedleys, or for that matter of the King himself, on account of Pepys' otherwise sober and discreet character; they can be noted with much more amusement and sympathy than a modern student can spare for aristocratic rakes who at most wrote a comedy or two in the intervals of fornication. Samuel sandwiched the spices of his own un-sanctified sexual pleasures between solid layers of hard office work and real matrimonial devotion.

But this world, gorgeous at the top, sordid at the bottom, socially and scientifically, if not morally, progressive, swept simultaneously by sea breezes and the perfumes of the alcove, could also be dangerous. It held dangers, in particular, for an ambitious young man intent on getting much further up in it than he was at present.

The state of the country had been gravely disturbed ever since the death of Oliver Cromwell in 1658. The dictator had nominated his eldest son, Richard, to succeed him. As Richard was not a military man, having lived most of his thirty-two years as a mere country squire, he was not popular with the all-powerful army and in the spring of 1659 the Army forced the new Protector to dissolve Parliament. The army officers set up a council of their own to govern the country, as regularly happens in history when the founder of a new regime dies or falls. Richard capitulated to this sovereignty of the sword, retiring into private life.

Royalist reaction spread, as it is spreading in 1958 in Spain, where a somewhat similar situation has recently developed. In the England of 1659 more and more people came to believe that a restoration of the monarchy in the person of Charles, the exiled eldest son of the king who had been beheaded by his subjects ten years before, could alone avoid the horrors of yet another civil war. General Monk, commander-in-chief of the forces holding Scotland, began an unopposed march to London. No one quite knew what he meant to do. Perhaps he was not yet quite sure himself. The so-called 'Rump Parliament'—the fag-end of its predecessors—was sitting, though somewhat apprehensively. Samuel merely comments in his Diary, on the 9th January 1660: 'I heard for certain that Monk was coming to London and that Bradshaw's lodgings were preparing for him.'

John Bradshaw, former President of the Council of State, had died the previous year, so it seemed that Monk was to take his place. On the other hand, the situation was obscure, with powerful republicans still trying to hold the ground that the royalists were steadily gaining. Samuel himself knew little and cared less about politics at this time. So long as he kept his post, he did not much mind who ruled the country. However, men in even comparatively humble positions were falling with startling rapidity if they got the reputation of being inconvenient to the more exalted. Nothing is more inconvenient than an eccentric chatterbox, and Sam did not intend to have that label pasted on him if he could help it.

So this Diary—he could no longer resist the temptation to keep one—was to be secret, a secret he would carry with him to the grave. He did so carry it, for it was not until 1818 that the Master of Magdalene College, Cambridge, to which establishment Pepys, a former sizar of it, had bequeathed his books, decided to publish the six volumes of shorthand. By 1822 they had been deciphered, and a first and partial edition appeared in 1825. But it was only at the end of the nineteenth century that the whole Diary was given to the world—with the exception, wrote its editor, Dr. H. B. Wheatley, of 'a few passages which cannot possibly be printed'. We shall see in due course what can be made of these tactful omissions.

Sam's prudence had been learned long before he made that first entry, dated 1st January 1660, in his very private journal. The metaphorical field of wild oats is the best of all possible schools for the absorption of that lesson. There had been women and there had been wine for his more boyish years; not to mention the ladies for the moment, a memorandum by the Registrar of Magdalene College, dated 21st October 1653, notes that 'Peapys and Hind were solemnly admonished by myself and Mr. Hill for having been scandalously over-served with drink ye night before. This was done in the presence of the Fellows then resident, in Mr. Hill's chamber'.

Sam was then twenty. The family was an old one, going back to the thirteenth century. By the sixteenth they were recognised gentry, with a coat of arms, but John Pepys, the diarist's father, had gone into trade, as the younger sons of gentlemen often did in those days. He was a tailor, not a very successful one, and he had moreover married a woman of inferior social rank, the sister of a butcher; but he could afford to give Sam, the second son of a large family, a good education. The boy was sent to St. Paul's School and to Magdalene as a 'sizar', which meant that he got his 'size', i.e. food, free. He received certain other emoluments, so that the average under-graduate of the day no doubt despised him. Yet the paternal allowance could not have amounted to very much, and opportunities for those 'wild oats' would thus be limited, though as we have seen Sam did not go short of wine. More-over, the contemporary Cambridge girls, despite the official puritanism of the 1650s, may be assumed to have been not much less free and easy, at any rate where university men were concerned, than they had been ten years before, during the hectic period of the Civil War.

'Peeps', as the family name was always pronounced, took his B.A. degree in 1654. That his amorous proclivities were well in evidence by that time is proved by the fact that as an undergraduate he wrote a play, which he afterwards destroyed, with the significant title *Love Is A Cheat*. One need not suppose that he had been particularly unlucky, but it may well be that this vanished literary effort records a disillusioning step in his progress to the prudence of 1660.

On 1st December 1655 Samuel Pepys, though still without regular employment, married a certain Elizabeth St. Michel, aged fifteen, the pretty but poverty-stricken daughter of a Frenchman who had accompanied Queen Henrietta Maria to England in 1625, on her marriage to King Charles I. The Sieur de St. Michel subsequently married an Irish widow, saw active service against the Spaniards and was delighted, as a

Protestant himself, with his daughter's betrothal to so 'religious' a man—so she herself had proclaimed him and so he had no doubt proclaimed himself to her—as Mr. Samuel Pepys, late of Magdalene College, Cambridge.

Elizabeth's physical attractions were quite considerable, though not outstanding. She was about Samuel's own height and had what the seventeenth century and her husband in particular, as we shall see, greatly admired, viz. rather full and prominent breasts. The ordinary workaday costume for young women at this period, to say nothing of more elaborate kit, emphasised the feature in question, with the result that girls well endowed in this respect were usually married off in their teens, with or without dowries. A slender waist and the ability to dress well when she had the chance enabled Elizabeth to cut a very good figure on her wedding-day.

Her taste for finery, though Samuel shared it and it was modified by her innate gift for dressmaking, gave her new husband many anxious moments as time went on, for he was by no means a prodigal spender, even at a later date, when he could well afford it. There were other drawbacks to be noted in Elizabeth, too. She was not very well educated, though she could write after a fashion and read light novels. She chattered a lot, had an inexhaustible appetite for entertainments, preferably in the company of her busy husband, and, worst of all, her temper was furious and unpredictable, though as a rule short-lived, especially in the first years of her marriage.

Samuel had fallen deeply in love with her. He never varied in his heartfelt devotion to his wife, though his physical infidelities, the main subject of this study, were numerous and constant. Elizabeth herself was flirtatious, but really virtuous. Samuel was often jealous of her; but so far as can be ascertained from the Diary he never had a genuine cause for jealousy. On the other hand, her own very well-founded jealousy of him far exceeded his, and was a perpetual torment to him. In the end it struck him a staggering blow, from which his amorous tendencies never really recovered; but that time was not yet. The course of true love in this very special case—for Elizabeth was actually as much in love with Samuel as he was with her, yet as prudish at heart as he was the opposite—could only be doomed to a rough passage. The miracle is that for fourteen years, in fact to the very day of her death, they got on as well together as they did.

It was lucky for Sam that his father-in-law, from whom Elizabeth inherited her good looks, was a rather reckless and eccentric character—so was his daughter, within certain well-defined limits—who did not care much about money, for the newly-weds had no prospects at all, apart from the possible good offices of the husband's distant cousin, Admiral Sir Edward Montagu. This gentleman, some eight years older than Samuel and already an officer of some distinction under the Protectorate, had probably helped John Pepys with the education of the latter's most promising son. Montagu was an honest and carelessly good-natured man, as well as able and courageous, himself on the up-grade, having been made a 'general-at-sea', as admirals were then called, the year after Sam's marriage.

The young couple, both of them as charming as they were penniless, actually managed to persuade Sir Edward to receive them as guests in his own quarters in Whitehall, the administrative as opposed to the commercial centre of London. Montagu made, however, the condition that Sam should occasionally act as his agent in official business. Both men soon had reason to be very well satisfied with this arrangement. Sam proved discreet and hard-working, and just then Montagu needed both qualities in a confidential employee. Everybody knew that Oliver Cromwell, though not yet sixty and at the height of his power and glory, could not last much longer; he was ageing fast after an exceptionally strenuous career, marked in its last years by recurrent illness. Nobody could guess what might happen when he died and an ambitious admiral had to provide for all possible contingencies.

On 26th March 1660, Sam writes in the famous Diary: 'This day it is two years since it pleased God that I was cut of the stone' (i.e. successfully operated on for calculus in the kidney) 'at Mrs. Turner's in Salisbury Court' (Pepys was born at a house in this Court, which is near St. Bride's churchyard, where his father had the tailor's shop). 'And did resolve,' he goes on, 'to keep it a festival, as I did the last year at my house, and for ever to have Mrs. Turner and her company with me.' This Mrs. Turner was Sam's cousin Jane, the wife of a lawyer. We shall hear more of her, especially of her legs, which were much admired by the Diarist.

Sam had little more trouble with his kidneys, except in cold weather, when he had, as the Diary notes on 26th March 1664, 'pain in making water, by gathering of wind and growing costive—' while 'upon the least squeeze almost my cods' (testicles) 'begin to swell and come to great pain, which is very strange and troublesome to me, though upon the speedy applying of a poultice it goes down again and in two days I am well'.

The anniversaries of this important surgical operation were always occasions on which Pepys took stock of his health, which was pretty good as a rule. But in 1665 he writes: 'A week or two ago I had one day's great pain; but it was upon my getting a bruise on one of my testicles and then I did void two small stones, without pain though, and upon my going to bed and bearing up of my testicles I was well the next.' Fortunately for a man of Sam's sanguine temperament this is about the sum total of injuries to the more private parts of his person. A large proportion of the population in that age of sexual recklessness and speculative medicine were by no means so lucky. The other great diarist of the time, John Evelyn, tells us, incidentally, that Pepys showed to Evelyn's brother Richard the 'stone' of which Sam himself was 'cut' in 1658, and that it was 'as big as a tennis ball'. No less than seven calculi were found in his left kidney when he died at the age, quite advanced for those days, of seventy-one.

In 1659 Sir Edward Montagu was sent by Richard Cromwell, the new Protector, to the Cattegat, as England's representative at the forthcoming peace negotiations between Sweden and Denmark. Pepys accompanied his patron in the flagship of the fleet, the *Naseby*, named after the decisive battle in 1645 of the

recent civil war. The Admiral was by this time one of the many
prominent republican officers in England who had come to
favour a Stuart restoration. He got into touch with the exiled
Court in Belgium, then under Spanish protection; but it was
not until 7th November 1660, a few months after Sir Edward
had been created Earl of Sandwich by his grateful king, that
the earl's former agent first heard, from his lordship's own
lips, what had been going on under his very nose aboard the
Naseby.

Sam, nothing if not secretive himself, was much impressed
by his cousin's discretion, and no doubt resolved to imitate
it—not necessarily in high policy, but certainly in those little
passing interludes with the other sex which so often came the
way of highly susceptible and mobile young men, whether
married or not, in the seventeenth century. The Admiral had
taught him one of the most profitable lessons which a budding
Don Juan can learn.

On the return of the fleet to England, Pepys was appointed,
through his patron's influence, to the Treasury clerkship
already mentioned, in which he was concerned with the pay of
the Army. Soon afterwards he made his first entry in the great
and carefully ciphered Diary. He was then living in Axe Yard,
near King Street, Westminster, a house of his own at last, with
his pretty wife and one maidservant, 'in very good health' and
with every prospect of success in his career under Sir Edward's
wing.

I

Kissing and Stocktaking

WRITERS on the social history of the English middle class in the seventeenth century, especially the Cromwellian period, often tend to stress the general piety and formality of manners. Church-going and ceremony certainly did take up a good deal of the time of ordinary people of this sort, but relaxation was apt to be boisterous even before the Restoration introduced a gaiety which lost much of its ebullience under Dutch William and Queen Anne. In the afternoon of 24th January 1660, a scene took place at the house of a certain 'Mr. Pierce' which even shocked the amorous Mr. Samuel Pepys, to say nothing of his more straight-laced young wife.

It is probable, though not certain, that this Pierce was the already prominent surgeon Dr. James Pierce, of whose very pretty wife we shall hear more, for Sam was much interested in her and her prosperous, gay and up-to-date circle. But whoever 'Mr. Pierce' may have been, he was no great stickler for the conventions. He had asked Mr. and Mrs. Pepys to 'dinner', a midday meal in the seventeenth century, where they found their fellow guests to be Mrs. Carrick, a very smartly dressed lady whom Pepys never met again, and one Mr. Lucy, also very smart, whom Sam then recognised for the first time as one of his many rivals for the favours of Mrs. Pierce.

'They called one another husband and wife,' writes the Diarist of the Carrick-Lucy team, 'and after dinner a great deal of mad stir. There was pulling of Mrs. Bride's and Mr. Bridegroom's ribbons, with a great deal of fooling among them that I and my wife did not like. Mr. Lucy and several other gentlemen coming in after dinner swearing and singing as if they were mad . . .'

This 'pulling of ribbons' was part of a favourite and often very licentious game of the period, entitled 'Husbands and Wives'. It consisted essentially of a burlesque of the traditional ceremony, by then already rather out of fashion in London, of undressing the bridegroom after a wedding. The process was also, needless to say, applied to the bride. Though perhaps it did not go so far as the twentieth century 'strip poker', it undoubtedly led to a good many unexpected revelations and shrieks of embarrassment, coupled in all probability with various other improprieties. In fact, it was often, and evidently on this occasion, a kind of minor orgy. At any rate young Sam and his Elizabeth were scandalised, though if the latter had not been present the former might have been as enterprising as anybody.

If social manners were sometimes on the crude side, political manners were cruder still. Since Cromwell's death Parliament had come into extremely bad odour. Its nickname of the 'Rump', applied ten years before, was now taken quite literally. Early in February 1660, writes the Diarist, 'Mr. Moore told me of a picture hung up at the Exchange of a great pair of buttocks shooting of a turd into Lawson's mouth and over it was wrote, "The thanks of the House". Boys do now cry, "Kiss my Parliament!" instead of "Kiss my arse!", so great and general a contempt is the Rump come to among all the good and bad'. Lawson was the Admiral of that name prominent in political life at the time. He assisted in escorting Charles to England a few months later.

General Monk was by this time in London with his army. 'We saw all his forces march by in very good plight and stout officers . . . the Parliament House was most of them with Monk at Whitehall . . . in his passing through the town he had many calls to him for a free Parliament, but little other welcome . . . the country being all discontented.'

The General visited the House on 6th February and found that there was little to stop him doing anything he pleased. A day or two later he called the City merchants, who were naturally enough opposed to another military Government, sharply to order by arresting some of their Common Council, pulling down their ancient fortifications and sequestering their Charter. Monk, a heavy, slow speaking man, was a good diplomatist. The City soon changed its tune, and rallied behind him against the Parliament. Then the astute General conciliated the latter by declaring himself in favour of a continuation of the Commonwealth and against having any dealings with Charles Stuart. George Monk (or Monck) may have been of Dutch extraction, though he was born in Devonshire. He certainly resembled a typical Dutchman in his ponderous physique, equable temperament and ingenious, not to say, tortuous, business sense. He was one of those who are always generally respected, even when they make mistakes, for the very reason that such men are never brilliant. Both Charles I and Cromwell had found him a soldier of the greatest possible discretion and steadiness of mind. After fighting for the former in the Civil War he had been captured in 1644 and imprisoned in the Tower for two years. The victorious Parliament then released him to serve it in Ireland and later in Scotland. He had been a great help to Cromwell at the battle of Dunbar in 1651, from which Prince Charles, Monk's future king and patron, had fled into exile.

Monk proceeded to serve the Commonwealth as a 'general at sea' against the Dutch, in successful association with one of the greatest of English admirals, Robert Blake. In 1653 he returned to Scotland, administering that country for the next five years with such characteristic caution that neither the Protector in England nor Prince Charles on the Continent quite knew whether the General really favoured a permanent republic or a restoration of the monarchy. He certainly refused to listen to Charles in 1659, and yet in January 1660, as we have seen, he led his army across the Tweed with an object which no one could guess at the time. Probably, as already suggested, he himself had not yet made up his mind at this date.

Sir Edward Montagu, Samuel heard to his great satisfaction

on 29th February, was already on excellent terms with the new arbiter of the fate of the nation, and had been appointed 'General at Sea', i.e. commander-in-chief of the fleet. Monk certainly knew how to get on well with everybody, though he may not have suspected at this time that Sir Edward was a royalist. The point for General Monk was that Montagu was immensely popular with the seamen, who were, understandably enough in the conditions of the time, difficult to please; since England's naval power was rising rapidly, the seamen formed an important part of the armed forces of the country. The omnipotent General needed a first-rate subordinate at the head of the potentially dangerous navy. Monk was finding it hard enough to control the landsmen, his own troops, loyal though they were to him and strongly opposed to Charles Stuart. But, strangely enough, Parliament was now beginning to favour a return of the exiled Prince.

It was in this connection that Pepys made a great stride forward in his professional career. On 23rd March 1660 he went aboard the *Swiftsure* as secretary to Sir Edward Montagu, bound for Charles' continental headquarters. The expedition's business took Montagu and his cousin to Holland, where Sam accompanied Mr. John Creed, Deputy Treasurer to the Fleet and decidedly a ladies' man, on an adventurous jaunt ashore. 'Mr. Creed and I went in the fore part of a coach wherein were two very pretty ladies, very fashionable and with black patches, who very merrily sang all the way and that very well and were very free to kiss the two blades that were with them.'

It was unfortunate that these lively Dutch girls were escorted on that occasion. Neither did Sam have much luck in the Voorhout, the principal street of The Hague, 'where the ladies in the evening do as our ladies do in Hide Park. But for my life I could not find one handsome, but their coaches very rich and themselves so too.' This note sounds a little wistful. Perhaps it was Sam's pocket rather than his fastidious taste, of which there is not much evidence elsewhere apart from his own assertions, which forbade him to get to know these very grand Dutch courtesans a little better.

Next day he tried hard to get on terms with what seemed a less expensive proposition, 'a pretty sober Dutch lass' encountered 'by water', i.e. in a conveyance on one of the canals. But the more he talked, the more she read her book. 'I could not fasten any discourse upon her.' Eventually, however, he went with two other Englishmen—'both physicians', he adds significantly, implying that these medical men would do their best to preserve him from any unpleasant consequences—'to a Dutch house, where there was an exceedingly pretty lass, and right for the sport, but it being Saturday we could not have much of her company, but however I staid with them till 12 at night'.

But this success does not appear to have stimulated our still bashful traveller to any great extent; for next day, at an inn, 'I went to lie down in a chamber in the house, where in another bed there was a pretty Dutch woman in bed alone, but though I had a month's mind' (i.e. longed, as an eight months pregnant woman is supposed to) 'I had not the boldness to go to her. So there I slept an hour or two. At last she rose and then I rose and walked up and down the chamber, and saw her dress herself after the Dutch dress and talked to her as much as I could and took occasion, from her ring which she wore on her first finger, to kiss her hand, but had not the face to offer anything more. So at last I left her there and went to my company.' In England, we may be sure, this meeting would have had a more interesting sequel. The Dutch lady seems to have been a cool hand, and probably thought the respectable Englishman a bit of a prude. In this opinion she would, of course, have been vastly mistaken.

By April Admiral Sir Edward Montagu, representing the British Parliament, had come to terms with Charles and offered to bring him to England forthwith. The exiled king was one of those tall, dark and handsome men so often referred to by fortune-tellers. He was twenty-nine years old, physically very active and fond of all outdoor sports, including seamanship. As to indoor sports, everyone knew that he was insatiably addicted to fornication; but he ate sparingly, rarely drank to excess and was most amiable and considerate to those about him, including, of course, his mistresses. Witty, gay and a remorseless enemy to hypocrisy and fraud, he seemed cut out to be a good king by seventeenth-century standards.

Parliament, after hearing his promises of a general amnesty, religious freedom and full arrears of pay to the army, proclaimed him king on 8th May.

On 25th May 1660 Sam saw Charles land at Dover but did not himself get ashore—at Deal—until 8th June. At a tavern in Gravesend 'a good handsome wench I kissed, the first that I have seen a great while . . . weary and hot to bed . . .' He reached London next day, but was so busy with Sir Edward that he did not see his wife until the 10th. He had missed her greatly, and the reunion no doubt compensated for a less than glorious love-life in Holland; but within the month he was dancing attendance upon a celebrated beauty, Frances Butler, though apparently without any great success. It may be added that Mrs. Pepys was suffering from a mysterious internal complaint, which lasted for some time during that summer.

On 18th June Sir Edward, who was about to be created an earl for his services in bringing the King to Dover, but was still hesitating over the choice of title, told his cousin Sam that he was trying to get him appointed Clerk of the Acts, i.e. secretary to the Navy Board. This body was a civilian department, concerned with victualling and other supplies and the maintenance of the dockyards. The Navy Board offices were situated between Crutched Friars and Seething Lane, slightly north-west of the Tower, so as to be near the chief supply and repair yards at Deptford and Woolwich.

The Admiralty itself was then as now in Whitehall, and was headed by James, Duke of York, Charles' younger brother, as Lord High Admiral. It dealt with matters relating to command, strategy and naval construction. The ships were built mostly at Chatham and Portsmouth; Admiralty orders for the maintenance of personnel and materials were passed on to the Navy Board for administration. The Board appointed subordinate officers, placed contracts and kept records; it had seven members, viz. four principal officers and three commissioners, the latter representing the Admiralty. The offices included accommodation for the staff.

On 13th July Samuel obtained his patent of appointment and showed his wife where they were going to live. They moved in on the 17th. He had already met the principal officers and commissioners, some of whom he liked and some of whom he did not much care for. Sir George Carteret, Treasurer of the Navy, was a good-natured, handsome man with whom he was to be friends for many years. Colonel Slingsby, the Comptroller, was also a decent fellow, interested in literature; but he was to die, apparently of influenza, only just over a year later. Admiral Sir William Batten, the third principal officer—Pepys himself was to be the fourth—did not make such a good impression.

Batten, a fat little man with coarse features, had a rather peculiar history. He was of humble birth, but had made his name as a seaman on the Parliamentary side in the Civil War. In 1643 Queen Henrietta Maria, wife of Charles I, was returning to England aboard a Dutch man-of-war, with a large sum of money she had raised on the continent for the royal cause. Batten did his duty, knowing the Queen was aboard, by chasing and firing on the vessel, which, however, he failed to capture.

He then proceeded, it may be thought, to exceed his duty by firing shot after shot into the house in Bridlington Quay, Yorkshire, where he knew that Henrietta had taken refuge, forcing her to escape into the open. For this dubious exploit he was promoted to admiral. Later on he changed sides and took his ship to Holland to serve the exiled Court; he was thus in high favour at the Restoration, when he had received his knighthood as well as the post which he now occupied. Samuel detected a clumsy arrogance in his dress and demeanour, and expected to have trouble with him. In due course his expectation was fulfilled.

The commissioners were Lord John Berkeley, whom Pepys was to find a noisy, garrulous fellow, not altogether to be trusted; Mr. Peter Pett, a shipbuilder whom, as the only other commoner on the Board, Samuel at first liked, though he afterwards turned out a rogue; and finally Admiral Sir William Penn, with whom and whose family Samuel was to have a great deal to do in the years ahead.

Penn, father of the future Quaker founder of Pennsylvania, had been knighted for going with Sir Edward to Holland. He was a big, heavily-built man of thirty-nine, though he looked older, with a sanguine complexion and an intimidating set of oaths. He looked in fact a typical weather-beaten veteran, jovial and easy to get on with, but to Samuel his grey eyes appeared a bit shifty behind the broad grin. The prudent secretary determined to watch Sir William closely. He was to have plenty of opportunity to do so.

Sam engaged a boy of seventeen, one Will Hewer, to be his chief clerk. To begin with, he was not too favourably impressed; the lad seemed a bit awkward and lazy. Still, he was not bad-looking, had fairly refined features and might be trained in time to be a good servant. The training was really to take time, and make Sam lose his temper more than once. But Will Hewer stuck to him to the very last.

On Sunday, 12th August 1660, Mr. Pepys renewed his acquaintance with a person very important to his inner man, one who will figure largely in the extracts from his Diary to be quoted in these pages. She was a girl named Betty Lane, who kept a linen stall in Westminster Hall, as the shopping district surrounding that august edifice was generally called. Samuel kept up his association with her throughout the period of the Diary, despite various disputes and her marriage in 1664 to a disreputable purser named Martin. 'I took her to my Lord's' (i.e. Sir Edward Montagu's house) 'and did give her a bottle of wine in the garden, where Mr. Fairbrother of Cambridge did come and found us and drank with us. After that I took her to my house' (presumably the other Betty, Mrs. Pepys, was out) 'where I was exceeding free in dallying with her and she not unfree to take it.'

It would be interesting to know, a little more clearly than can be understood from the Diary, just what Betty Lane looked like. Her character is clear enough—what there was of it; to use an expression much in fashion some years ago, she was just 'a little bit of nonsense'. If we had a better idea of her physical type we should have a better one of Sam's taste in women, for it was to Betty Lane that he returned most often, whatever mood he was in.

The Diary only relates that her thighs were rather ample and her skin white. It is a fair conjecture that she was high-bosomed, for Samuel was most particular about this feature, as his choice of a permanent partner and his constant eulogies of this endowment in other female companions sufficiently show. Probably she was not a brunette, for the Diarist usually notes this colouring in women, which he preferred. It was fashionable at Court, though Charles' mistresses—a dark man's selection— were generally fair. For the rest, Betty Lane's appearance must be left to the imagination.

No doubt Mr. Pepys, like the majority of highly sexed young men, did not specialise, but went indiscriminately for all girls so long as they were, broadly speaking, 'pretty', a favourite word of his, probably meaning no more than gay, smart and appealing in a general sort of way. We do know that he was inclined to be shy of the heroic type, Amazonian or Junoesque. He notes their charms with respect, but rarely more. We may conclude that on the whole he preferred to associate with people of his own size or in a lighter class, a fairly common aim with Lotharios of his mercurial cast.

He could not leave the ladies alone, even during his mother's serious illness in early September of this year. 'My wife went this afternoon to see my mother, who I hear is very ill, at which my heart is very sad. In the afternoon Luellin' (a fellow civil servant) 'comes to my house and takes me out to the Mitre in Wood Street' (where an uproarious mixed party was being held, apparently in a private room). 'They were very merry, Luellin being drunk, and I being to defend the ladies from his kissing them, I kissed them myself very often with a great deal of mirth. Parted very late . . .'

On 22nd September, two days before Samuel Pepys was made a Justice of the Peace, he was drinking in the morning, a regular habit of our hero's, with that same Luellin. 'Among other discourse here he told me how the pretty woman that I always loved at the beginning of Cheapside, that sells childs' coats, was served by the Lady Bennett' (a famous strumpet, called 'Lady' by the wits in mere irony) 'who by counterfeiting to fall into a swoon upon the sight of her in her shop, became acquainted with her and at last got her ends of her to lie with a gentleman that had hired her to procure this poor soul for him. To Westminster to my Lord's and there in the house of office' (the privy) 'vomited up all my breakfast, my stomach being ill at this day by reason of the last night's debauch . . . I staid here all day in my Lord's chamber and upon the leads gazing upon Diana' (a complaisant neighbour whom he had seduced earlier in the month) 'who looked out of a window upon me. At last I went out . . . and she standing over the way at the gate I went over to her and appointed to meet tomorrow in the afternoon at my Lord's.' This appointment was not, however, kept by his scatter-brained acquaintance.

Pepys seemed to do much as he pleased at his 'Lord's'. In fact the earl himself, who had now chosen the title of Sandwich, was a jolly fellow, somewhat cynical in matters of sex and 'very indifferent in all matters of religion'. In discussing the Duke of York's notorious seduction of Anne Hyde, Lord Clarendon's daughter, whom the Duke at first refused to marry, though she was pregnant and the King said he ought to do so, Sandwich 'told me that among his father's many old sayings that he had wrote in a book of his, this is one, that he that do get a wench with child and marry her afterwards is as if a man should—' the Diarist here uses the common monosyllable for 'excrete' '—in his hat and then clap it on his head . . . my Lord makes nothing of these things.' This passage in the Diary ends with some sharp criticisms of services and sermons in West-minster Abbey, 'by my troth a pitiful sorry devotion . . .' Sam, unlike his 'Lord', was deeply attentive to at least the outward show of religious orthodoxy.

By 3rd November he was after Betty Lane again. 'To Westminster Hall, where I met with Tom Doling and we two took Mrs. Lane to the alehouse, where I made her angry with commending of Tom Newton and her new sweetheart to be both too good for her, so that we parted with much anger, which made Tom and me good sport.' Betty was evidently flirtatious, and it sounds as though Sam were jealous, though he pretended to be amused. However, by January 1661 he was discussing amicably with a friend named Hawley that gentleman's chances of a renewed assault on Betty's virtue. The shopgirls who played so large a part in the lives of men in Pepys' position—married and mixing with important courtiers—were not, of course, taken too seriously by their lovers, though sometimes the girls could and did cause serious trouble themselves.

In that same January Sam caught the other Betty, his wife, being kissed by a Frenchman at the table of a Mrs. Hunt, when he called there unexpectedly. Such a courtesy at mealtimes was a common enough practice in the seventeenth century in England; most foreign travellers in the island had noted this custom ever since the time of Erasmus, a hundred years before, and all of them, including no doubt the Frenchman in question, found the habit very agreeable.

Pepys remarks that he 'did not like' this episode, but adds, 'there could not be any hurt in it', which proves that such manners were acceptable enough at the period, even when perfect strangers were concerned.

There is a considerable difference between kissing and spitting, though these operations are performed with the same organs. But Samuel was not in the least incommoded when, one night at the theatre 'I sitting behind in a dark place a lady spit backward upon me by a mistake, not seeing me, but after seeing her to be a very pretty lady, I was not troubled by it at all'. He had been shocked, however, the previous year, when in the King's presence 'old Lady Middlesex' had had a serious accident with her bowels which everybody noticed. If Charles had not been there this little *contretemps* apparently would not have mattered.

The number of occasions recorded in the Diary when Mr.

Samuel Pepys, while staying at or visiting an inn or tavern, 'saw the girl of the house, being very pretty . . . and went and kissed her . . .' are legion. It is true that within living memory barmaids and chambermaids, like film actresses today, were engaged mainly for their looks, in the belief that they would attract custom, which in the overwhelming majority of cases they did. Up to 1914 they were often what Sam calls 'ripe for the sport' into the bargain. But from the point of view of Don Juan there was a sad falling off in the new world that was born about 1920. By then, girls had something better to do than yield their charms to one commercial or uncommercial traveller after another; in the seventeenth century, however, such 'maids' expected nothing else, and some of them made quite a good thing out of it without descending to the shame of the 'streets'. Their complaisance was all part of what we should now designate 'service', and no one concerned had the least twinges of conscience about it, let alone felt indignation. In the rest of this little study, therefore, there will be no need to dwell on these trivial episodes, in which Mr. Pepys was really not much more distinguished than the rest of his coevals.

But, as already mentioned, kissing one's social equals was also in high favour at this period, and there are nearly as many allusions to this amusement in the Diary as to the other. During an excursion on the Thames by barge with three ladies whom Samuel had only met for the first time that morning, he managed to induce them to go into the 'lanthorn', presumably a narrow closet in which the vessel's lantern was kept, followed them in 'and kissed them, demanding it as a fee due to a principall officer, with all which we were exceeding merry . . .' The next day he visited the same ladies and 'I staid there till 2 o'clock in the morning and was most exceeding merry and I had the opportunity of kissing Mrs. Rebecca' (who had shown him the most favour) 'very often. Among other things Captain Pett' (a naval officer present) 'was saying that he thought that he had got his wife with child since I came thither. Which I took hold of and was merrily asking him what he would take to have it said for my honour that it was of my getting? He merrily answered that he would if I would promise to be godfather to it if it did come within the time just and I said that I would. So that I must remember to compute it when the time comes.'

This sort of jesting was not that of a reckless and dissipated *coterie*, such as might be found in twentieth century Montmartre or Chelsea, but of two conscientious and well-educated servants of the State, both honourable and devoted husbands according to the standards of the age. The jokes would be considered in poor taste if made in a gentleman's house today, but to the seventeenth century mind nothing that raised a laugh was in bad taste.

The year 1661 was not one in which the amorous proclivities of the Clerk of the Acts had very free play. He was involved in a tremendous lot of official and family business. The King was crowned in April. Barbara Palmer—'My Lady Castlemaine'—the most beautiful madcap in England, was already Charles' mistress. The atmosphere at Court was both poverty-stricken and debauched; Parliament was restive, and the international horizon dark. Great numbers of Pepys' relatives seemed to die this year, and there were endless disputes about wills. His wife's health was not good, in common with that of many Londoners at the time, and he had reason more than once to suspect, though only to suspect, her fidelity. Sam himself had continual colds and headaches, the former causing his natural functions to give him a good deal of pain and the latter causing him, like Omar Khayyam, to forswear wine over and over again. Of course, he no more kept his vow than did the Persian poet.

He had discovered that hardly one of his professional colleagues was on really good terms with another, though in public they all pretended to be so. With the Penns he had already become fairly intimate, though he considered the household badly managed and the meals shocking. Sir William was not so bad, but Lady Penn stood absurdly on her dignity, while as for the children, William, the future founder of Pennsylvania, then at Oxford, seemed pious and dull, while

Peg, an ugly if precocious girl of fifteen, was all right for teasing, but nothing else.

The Battens he found frankly detestable, but naturally he never let them see it. Lady Batten was an even worse housekeeper than her neighbour Lady Penn, and was considerably more ill-mannered, smug and ignorant. Her daughter Martha tried to take after her, but did not succeed; while far from good-looking, she was really not a bad sort. Pepys felt sorry for her, but not otherwise interested.

He attended the coronation in April with these two families, since they all lived in adjoining buildings. As the King rode by he looked upwards at the Navy Board representatives gathered at the upper window of a shop, and gave them a special salute, with his characteristic broad grin. Samuel no doubt felt that it was a great moment.

For the rest of the year he kept as clear as he could, socially, of the Penns and Battens, alleging the perfectly true and valid excuse of pressure of business, above all the learning of his new and intricate job. When the Comptroller died, Sir John Minnes, another old sea-dog, replaced him. This admiral had a certain amount of charm. He was fond of medicine and chemistry; he loved Chaucer, as Pepys himself did, and was a good man at a party. He was much more cultured and amusing than either of the two Sir Williams. However, he was known to be a professional rival of Lord Sandwich, Sam's own patron and cousin. The Diarist had to steer an exceptionally prudent course in order to keep friendly with each of these magnates.

In June Sandwich had brought Catherine of Braganza from Portugal to marry Charles II. The earl received his young cousin amicably, and actually asked him to look after part of the new Queen's dowry for the time being. Lord Sandwich was in no hurry to pay it over to Charles, who had not yet reimbursed him his expenses for the voyage. Pepys locked the money up in his cellar for a few days, till the goldsmith's men —the bankers of the day—came to take it away.

It had been an anxious year; one of taking stock of his new position in society, settling down, learning new techniques of business and keeping Elizabeth from spending too much money, rather than of really enjoying himself. He often thought with regret of Westminster Hall and its gay inhabitants, but first things must come first, and the girls would simply have to wait for a while. Even now he was not sure whether he would be able to keep his head and his post amid so many dubious issues and conflicting interests.

Nevertheless, on 31st December he could write that he had four servants, two of each sex, comprising Will Hewer, a boy named Wayneman and two maids, Sarah and Nell, as well as a house at the Navy Office. As Clerk of the Acts, i.e. secretary or registrar of the Navy Board, he held a post of much responsibility, which he retained for the whole period of the Diary. Yet he knew nothing about the Navy when he entered upon his duties, and so little about accounts that he did not learn the multiplication table until July of the following year. But for all his wine-parties and kissing, the susceptible young man was a devilishly hard worker. In a few weeks he had been accepted as a model official; he was highly thought of by his patrons the Montagus—Lady Sandwich was devoted to both Sam and Elizabeth—and also by the majority of the important persons he dealt with.

'I suppose myself,' he goes on, 'to be worth about £500 clear in the world and my goods of my house my own and what is coming to me from Brampton' (he means his father's estate near Huntingdon) 'when my father dies, which God defer.' It was not a bad beginning, and was to improve beyond all Sam's expectations as time went on.

2

Frolics Away and at Home

IN April 1662, the Secretary paid an official visit to Portsmouth Dockyard, and was made a burgess of the town. 'After our work was done Sir G. Carteret' (Treasurer of the Navy), 'Sir W. Pen' (with whom Sam was very friendly at this time, though they afterwards quarrelled) 'and I walked forth and I spied Mrs. Pierce and another lady passing by. So I left them and went to the ladies and walked with them up and down and took them to Mrs. Stephen's' (where Carteret lodged) 'and there gave them wine and sweetmeats and were very merry. And then comes the Doctor' (Dr. Timothy Clerke, F.R.S.) 'and we carried them by coach to their lodging, which was very poor, but the best they could get and such as made much mirth among us. So I appointed one to watch when the gates of the town were ready to be shut and to give us notice; and so the Doctor and I staid with them playing and laughing and at last were forced to bid good night for fear of being locked into the town all night. So we walked to the yard' (i.e. the Dockyard) 'designing how to prevent our going to London to-morrow, that we might be merry with these ladies, which I did . . .'

This frolic was repeated the following day, lasting until midnight. Afterwards, at the Doctor's lodgings, 'our discourse being much about the quality of the lady with Mrs. Pierce, she being somewhat old and handsome and painted and fine and had a very handsome maid with her, which we take to be the marks of a bawd. But Mrs. Pierce says she is a stranger to her and met by chance in the coach and pretends to be a dresser. Her name is Eastwood.'

Mrs. Eastwood was still going strong four years later, when Sam met her again in London and much enjoyed her company, as we shall see in due course. Mrs. Pierce was of course a favourite of his already, and was well known to his wife, who naturally did not like her. Samuel always described her as a great beauty, though overpainted and no more a chicken than Mrs. Eastwood. At this period she already had two children. There is not much doubt, from the zestful though guarded language of the last entry, that both Pepys and Dr. Clerke carried matters to considerable lengths, probably each with both of these merry grass widows, at the Portsmouth meeting. Sam must have thanked his stars that he had managed to prevent Elizabeth from coming out with him from London. She had been determined upon it, and had been left at home in tears.

As for Dr. Clerke's wife, also left behind in London, the Secretary, on his return, called on her with a conjugal letter from his late crony. 'She is a very fine woman and what with her person and the number of fine ladies that were with her, I was much out of countenance and could hardly carry myself like a man among them. But however, I staid till my courage was up again . . .' It must have been with some surprise that a few years later he heard a story from no less a person than Mrs. Pierce herself, of this same 'mighty high, fine and proud' Mrs. Clerke soliciting a gentleman with success in Westminster Hall. 'Captain Rolt did see her the other day accost a gentleman in Westminster Hall and went with him and he dogged them to Moorefields to a little blind bawdy house and there staid watching three hours and they come not out, so could stay no longer but left them there and he is sure it was she, he knowing her well and describing her very clothes to Mrs. Pierce, which she knows are what she wears.'

In order to gain some insight into the mind of Mr. Samuel Pepys and through him into the mentality of average middle-class London in the seventeenth century, it is necessary to realise that people in those days had a very different outlook from our own on matters in which the sexual instinct is

concerned. In other fields, so many of the habits, thoughts and
feelings of the men and women of that time were practically
identical with those of the present day that it becomes hard
to believe in this one crucial distinction. Work and play,
gossip and more serious conversation, personalities the twins
of those which are always cropping up in the twentieth
century, as well as reactions to pleasure and pain, responsibility
and friendship or dislike, seem to have been about the same
then as they are now. But it would be exceptional even in the
eighteenth century, let alone the nineteenth or the twentieth,
for an important Government official and a Fellow of the
Royal Society, both genuinely devoted to their wives, to spend
several hours, while on a State visit to a provincial city, in
drinking and frolicking—to say the least of it—with two
married women, one at any rate of whom was on familiar
terms with one of the gentlemen's consorts.

The affair becomes even odder in modern eyes when we hear
that a year or two later one of the stay-at-home wives was seen
to solicit a man in the street and visit a brothel with him,
especially since the story is told without much comment, as if
it were a fairly common occurrence.

The fact is that young married women at the mid-level of
seventeenth-century society and girls of at least the lower
middle groups were quite as polyandrous, on the whole, as the
males were polygamously minded. For all their superficial
formality and piety, they considered they had just as much
right as the men to sexual fun and games, unlimited so long as
they were careful to preserve the appearances which everyone
knew had little to do with the reality. For of course divines
still thundered against the sin of concupiscence, and secular
critics who had never been found out themselves were still as
censorious as ever—in public.

It was an age when women, for the first time in English
history, were beginning to assert themselves. For instance, they
were appearing on the stage as freely as men, showing their
legs to, among so many others, that remarkably enthusiastic
playgoer Mr. Samuel Pepys, who heartily records his approval

of the custom, though also somewhat disapproving the almost invariably 'crooked hams' of these showgirls. Perhaps the new display of legs largely accounted for his very frequent visits to the theatre. He probably felt much the same exhilaration as did most of the males of the nineteen-twenties when very short skirts came into fashion.

Before the Civil War, though Queen Elizabeth—an exceptional person, of course—had once pulled up her farthingale in front of the French Ambassador, there had been no such emancipation of the gentler sex. Though the Civil War ended upon a note of puritanism, wars generally result, sooner rather than later, in increased freedom of manners and morals, and probably this development, deferred in the present case, had much to do with the 'golden' days of Charles II. The monarch at any rate liked a bold girl, as his taste in mistresses proved. 'If Barbara Palmer (later Lady Castlemaine), Frances Stuart, Nell Gwyn and the rest of them can climb so far by flouting the conventions, why not us?'—the wives of solid citizens and the daughters of small tradesmen may have thought—'What have the aristocrats and actresses got that we haven't?'

Consequently, while Charles reigned, sexual licence reached a height in London, at least, which it was never to regain (if we are to believe orthodox historians), except perhaps for a few years in the reign of Sigmund Freud, from about 1915— when the cure for syphilis was discovered—to 1928, when the sound film gave people something else to think about. The Caroline wave of erotic debauchery was exasperated, as the later one was not, or if at all much more slightly, by a feeling among women that they were avenging centuries of oppressive exploitation. Their masculine opposite numbers under King Charles therefore welcomed the new opportunities with mixed sentiments, as the regular *leit-motif* of Restoration literature, cuckoldry, sufficiently suggests. Generally the men reacted with an enhanced brutality, as it seems to modern minds. But the cynically cruel jeers and worse treatment which women then suffered, and from which the toughest modern dramatic critic now shrinks when he watches our relatively mildly-acted and discreetly produced revivals of them on the stage, did not mean that men were winning the sex war, the first they had ever had to fight. Till near the end of the century they had the worst of it, both in England and elsewhere.

Sam was not a front-line soldier in this campaign, but he was certainly in the thick of it. The peculiar character of his amorous behaviour, by turns recklessly hardened and timidly anxious, as we are apt to think on a first acquaintance with him, is to be judged in the light of that circumstance. Of course, something must be allowed for his extreme preoccupation with affairs in his strenuous professional career at this time. 'I find it a hard matter to settle to business after so much leisure and pleasure,' he writes plaintively on 6th May. For Samuel's appetite grew, as the Diary proves again and again, by what it fed on. He would have preferred to go straight from Portsmouth to Betty Lane; but instead of that he had to deal with Sir George Carteret.

The knight was in a temper, annoyed with Penn, who had suggested to the Duke of York—in pursuance of his intrigues against the other members of the Navy Board—that this body could do with another commissioner. The Duke was sending down William Coventry, his private secretary, in this capacity.

Pepys knew Coventry slightly, and liked him for his apparent honesty—which was in fact genuine—though here again, as often enough in other cases, he found the secretary rather cool towards Lord Sandwich, a circumstance which stood in the way of greater intimacy between Samuel and Coventry. Still, he was as glad as Sir George was sorry to hear that Coventry was coming. Samuel's orderly mind had already been offended by the ineffectual way in which business was conducted at the Navy Office. He himself had no authority to set matters right, but Coventry had. The Clerk of the Acts secretly wished him luck.

The average Don Juan is often a scapegrace, but Sam, though his 'amours'—as he called them—came near to rivalling those of Lord Rochester and Sir Charles Sedley, would never have dreamed of emulating the wild antics, mostly performed in the nude, of those typical Restoration rakes. On the contrary, he was almost as much concerned to regulate his amorous behaviour, in case it should land him in trouble, as he was to keep his accounts properly at the Office. He had plenty of examples before him of the disasters which, even in the golden days of Charles, too frenzied a devotion to the ladies might bring upon a public man. He was soon to find not even Lord Sandwich immune from them.

It was not only the atmosphere of that reckless age that accounted for Samuel's caution in love affairs, as in commercial ones. An amusing streak of puritanical peremptoriness mingled with his grosser lusts. He rode his mistresses with a tight rein once they had capitulated, and was sedulous in covering his own tracks to their alcoves. This combination of amorist and book-keeper, though not unknown in later periods, was rare in Mr. Pepys' day and certainly contributes to the piquancy of his memoirs.

He did his best to placate the furious Sir George, and assured him of his personal loyalty if Coventry started any hares; but after the knight had gone the hostility between Coventry and Sandwich, one a man of the Court who had never been anything else and the other a former Parliamentarian, began to worry the Clerk of the Acts. He owed everything to the earl, and he felt as instinctive a liking for the hot-tempered but honourable Carteret as he did for Coventry, with whom he had so far had less to do. It was a difficult situation. Once more the girls would have to wait awhile.

When Mr. Coventry arrived, tall and self-possessed, with perfect manners and an inscrutable expression, Samuel, after two meetings, believed he had made a good impression on the Duke of York's representative. He seemed to be right, for a few days later Coventry asked for his company on an official trip down the river to Woolwich. Aboard the barge the two men discussed Cicero, and the courtier complimented Mr. Pepys on his speeches at the two last conferences.

All through June the Clerk and the extra commissioner

constantly inspected the yards at Woolwich and Deptford together, rectifying abuses, listening to complaints and acquainting themselves with every detail of the work which went on there, Pepys standing up stoutly for the labourers and Coventry taking everything in with his permanent polite smile, attentive and sympathetic, if slightly wary. It was hard to make out what he was thinking. Then, in mid-July, he left England with the Duke of York to fetch the Queen Mother, Henrietta Maria, to her eldest son's Court.

That month there were workmen in Samuel's new house in Seething Lane. With some difficulty he managed to persuade his wife to go to the country for a couple of months until the place was fit to live in again. No sooner was her back turned than the Clerk of the Acts, who now slept at the neighbouring house of his friend Sir William Penn, just then in Ireland, began to make love to the latter's maid.

'God forgive me,' he writes on 1st August. 'I was sorry to hear that Sir W. Pen's maid Betty was gone away yesterday, for I was in hopes to have had a bout with her before she had gone, she being very pretty. I had also a mind' (he coolly adds) 'to my own wench, but I dare not for fear she should prove honest and refuse and then tell my wife . . .' Five days later—
'. . . can hardly keep myself from having a mind to my wench but I hope I shall not fall to such a shame to myself . . .'

This 'wench' was Jane Wayneman, sister of Pepys' original boy servant, whom he had dismissed two years before for theft. The lad's place had been taken in September 1660 by his brother, an unruly but not apparently dishonest youth, whom his master was obliged to thrash on several occasions. Yet he stayed for some three years, and it was not until the autumn of 1663 that he was finally shipped off to Barbados as hopeless.

The Waynemans were all rather wild, typical of the seventeenth century 'lower orders' in their boisterous humour, sharp tongues, excitable temperaments and general unreliability. Jane seems to have been engaged about the same time as her second brother. On 1st December 1660 Sam had also found it necessary to apply corporal punishment to her, 'basting' her with a broom for not doing her work properly 'till she cried extremely, which made me vexed, but before I went out I left her appeased'. She was a lively sort of girl. When Pepys called her in the middle of the night of the 27th of the same month, as he was feeling ill, 'she pleased my wife and I in her running up and down so innocently in her smock . . .' Later she cut off the moustache of one of the workmen in the house and was rude to Lady Batten, the Pepyses' next-door neighbour. Nothing much appears to have come of Sam's passing fancy for her, and it was not long before she was dismissed for 'some sauciness' to her mistress. Towards the end of September 1662 Mrs. Pepys returned from the country. 'I was very pleased to see her and after supper to bed and had her company with great content and much mutual love . . .' But the course of true love between Elizabeth and Samuel did not always run so smoothly.

Maidservants and less frequently manservants were often sources of disagreement between husbands and wives. In middle-class seventeenth century households, the domestic worker was usually far more of a member of the family than became the case later. He or she popped in and out of the matrimonial bedroom at all hours, and sometimes slept there. There were long periods when the master or mistress remained alone with an employee of the opposite sex, ostensibly at work, but as often as not gossiping. It was no wonder that sexual advantage was occasionally taken of these opportunities, mostly on the initiative of the person of higher social rank, though servants could be as impudent then as they never were again till the last decade before their final disappearance, *circa* 1930.

Mrs. Pepys again and again taxed her husband with trying out the maids, which he undoubtedly did sometimes, though never, it seems at this time, to any serious extent. As a rule he was too prudent a man to take chances in his own nest when there was so much easy game elsewhere. Moreover, he really did wish to keep on good terms with his wife; despite her quick temper and alternate fits of extravagance and cheese-paring. Elizabeth, like most girls with a touch of French blood

in them, was decidedly shrewd, and occasionally a real help
to her husband in his affairs. Without understanding business
in the least, she had plenty of common sense. The poor child's
health was not good, but at any rate she was virtuous, or much
more so than her husband. Sam bore with her tantrums
cheerfully and gave her no colourable excuse, by the standards
of the day, to renew them. He had the more reason for doing
so in that the physical relations between husband and wife
were perfectly satisfactory. The lady had 'temperament'. Sam
was for ever 'lying late' in bed with her, 'sporting with great
pleasure,' he writes on 24th October 1662, 'for we have been
for some years now and at present more and more a very
happy couple.'

On the whole, 1662 had been a good year for Samuel. As
regards his public career, not only had he been elected a
Younger Brother of Trinity House in February, but he had
also been appointed a member of no less a body than the
Tangier Commission. The port had been acquired as part of
the dowry of Catherine of Braganza, and was considered a
useful foothold in the Mediterranean. The commission was to
govern and fortify it. The Duke of York, Prince Rupert (who
was the King's cousin), General Monk (by now Duke of
Albemarle), Lord Sandwich, Lord Southampton, Sir George
Carteret and Mr. Coventry were all members.

It was Sandwich, of course, who had nominated Mr. Pepys,
but it was Coventry who had secured him the necessary votes
by stressing, in a Ciceronian speech, the 'diligence, integrity
and ability' of the Clerk of the Acts, adding, to Samuel's intense
delight, the phrase 'life of the Navy Office'.

The house at the Navy Office was now repaired and in 'good
condition', 'very convenient'. Sam was worth about £650 in
hard cash, more than the year before, and had certain 'goods
of all sorts' in the shape of furniture, clothes and so forth.
The only snag had been repeated troubles with servants and
relatives, as well as the fact, perhaps, that he had been obliged
to live 'a very orderly life all this year by virtue of the oaths
that God put into my heart to take against wine, plays and

other expenses', the last item no doubt accounting for the sparse extra-marital divagations of the Clerk of the Acts, Younger Brother of Trinity House and Tangier Commissioner during the last twelve months. But these good resolutions were not kept very much longer.

Stories of the Court were hardly calculated to set Sam a good example in his determination to stick to business and give 'pleasures' a wide berth. On the very first day of the new year he writes: 'In fine, I find that there is nothing almost but bawdry at Court from top to bottom.' Next month, though he had added that it was not necessary to 'give instances' of these goings on, he does so at considerable length. The passage runs:

'About a month ago, at a ball at Court, a child was dropped by one of the ladies in dancing, but nobody knew who, it being taken up by somebody in their handkercher . . . but it seems Mrs. Wells' (one of Queen's maids of honour) 'fell sick that afternoon and hath disappeared ever since, so that it is concluded that it was her.' Another story was how 'my lady Castlemaine, a few days since, had Mrs. Stuart' (known as 'la belle Stuart', the second greatest beauty at Charles' Court) 'to an entertainment and at night began a frolique that they two must be married and married they were, with ring and all other ceremonies of church service and ribbands and a sack posset in bed and flinging the stocking; but in the close it is said that my lady Castlemaine, who was the bridegroom, rose and the King came and took her place with pretty Mrs. Stuart . . .' Another story was how Captain Ferrers and 'W. Howe' (both wild fellows and intimate friends of the Diarist) 'both have often, through my lady Castlemaine's window, seen her go to bed and Sir Charles Barkeley' (a typical Restoration gallant, recklessly immoral, but very good-natured and brave as a lion) 'in the chamber all the while with her.' Barkeley was Captain of the King's Guard, and among other things, despite his usual amiability, a very strict disciplinarian. When Ferrers, also a Guardsman, on one occasion apologised to Sir Charles for a night's absence from barracks, his chief, 'swearing and cursing told him, before a great many other gentlemen, that he would not suffer any man of the King's Guards to be absent from his lodging a night without leave. Not but that, says he, once a week or so I know a gentleman must go —ing and I am not for denying it to any man, but however he shall be bound to ask leave to lie abroad and to give account of his absence that we may know what guard the King has to depend upon.' This incorrigible young Cavalier of the old school was killed, as the Earl of Falmouth, aboard the *Royal Charles*, at the battle of Lowestoft against the Dutch on 3rd June 1665, his blood bespattering the Duke of York, who was standing beside him.

The story of the dropped child had a sequel. 'The King had it in his closett a week after and did dissect it and making great sport of it said that it must have been a month and three hours old, and that, whatever others think, he hath the greatest loss (it being a boy, as he says) that hath lost a subject by the business.' These tales may not be true in every detail; but, as Samuel himself might have observed, there is no smoke without fire, and a sort of poetic if not literal truth seems to hang about such gossip. The King's jest is in character, and so is Lady Castlemaine's wild 'frolique', which probably does not indicate a 'Lesbian' streak in her, as the modern mind might well suppose. Much more probably it was pure mischievous high spirits.

Anyhow, the Diarist could not get the anecdote out of his head for some time, for he refers to it more than once later, and seems in fact to have brooded over it. There is plenty of evidence in his self-communings that Lady Castlemaine was his secret ideal.

Very soon after the Diarist's declaration of their conjugal happiness Samuel and Elizabeth began to fall out seriously. The reason was Elizabeth's boredom with her new social position as the wife of an extremely busy public figure, whose private preoccupations also led to some prolonged absences from the matrimonial hearth. Mrs. Pepys complained of having nothing to do at home on these occasions, and being too often deprived of the pleasure of going 'abroad' or, as we should say, 'out', with her husband.

She therefore requested to be allowed to engage a suitable feminine companion. In those days, as in later centuries, it was a common practice for lonely ladies who could afford it to take decently bred but impecunious young women into their houses for company. Although they occasionally helped in the house, their chief function was to dance attendance on their principals indoors and out unless and until they married or, as frequently happened, the husband or some other male relative or friend began to take too great an interest in them.

Samuel at first resisted this demand, both on economic and general grounds. He was afraid it would cost too much, and also that such a girl might well lead his only too lively wife into undesirable quarters. Elizabeth sulked furiously, and cut out her habit of lying in bed with him in the mornings for 'dalliance'. Mr. Pepys even held out against this dire assault upon his legitimate rights. Then, one day in February, his consort was robbed of a parcel in broad daylight, as she sat in a hackney coach in Cheapside, while the horse was being watered. If she had had a companion, she pointed out tearfully, this awful thing could never have happened.

Balthasar St. Michel, Elizabeth's brother, recommended first one girl and then another. The second candidate, Mary Ashwell, at that moment a school teacher in Chelsea, seemed very suitable. She was 'a pretty, ingenious girl at all sorts of fine work, which pleases me very well'. She could play well on the 'harpsicon' and the 'triangle', and in addition to her musical ear, danced better than her mistress and took a good hand at cards. In short, she was the best attendant, from Sam's point of view, that they had ever had. His wife was not so sure. A storm began to brew in this connection, but it did not burst for another month or two.

It was perhaps on account of Mary Ashwell's obvious conquest of Samuel that his wife began to take dancing lessons from a Mr. Pembleton, rather too many to please the Diarist. Matters reached a climax on the night of 15th May, when on returning home he found 'my wife and the dancing-master alone above, not dancing but talking. Now so deadly full of jealousy I am that my heart and head did so cast about and fret that I could not do any business possibly . . . (my wife) by her folly has too much opportunity given her with the man, who is a pretty neat, black' (i.e. dark-haired) 'man, but married. But it is a deadly folly and plague that I bring upon myself to be so jealous . . . I am ashamed to think what a course I did take by lying to see whether my wife did wear drawers to-day as she used to do and other things to raise my suspicion of her, but I found no true cause of doing it.'

It was rare at this period for the Diarist so to burn the paper with his self-tormentings; but his unusual agitation proves (*a*) that he really loved Elizabeth Pepys, and (*b*) that he knew from personal experience how easy it is for 'temperamental' people to slip from the straight and narrow path, if only for half an hour. It is obvious enough from other evidence that both he and his wife were highly sexed, and knew each other to be so. So far it was Sam who had given most cause for that jealousy which always flames highest in those who are sexually most demanding. But now it was Elizabeth who fed the flame.

Incidentally, the 'drawers,' to which the distracted husband refers, were not of course the glamorous garments of the late nineteenth century which lingered on so long into the twentieth that allusions to them can still raise a laugh or a gleam in the eye from old-fashioned people. They were sober, trouser-like affairs which ladies, as well as men, wore on certain occasions —when it was cold or when they felt that there might be a risk to their chastity—but by no means all the time. Mrs. Pepys, like her husband, was very subject to internal chills. Probably she had got into the habit of fortifying her health in this way to the extent that if she could be proved not to have done so on any particular day it might well be circumstantial evidence of an intention to commit adultery under conditions—as in an upper room of her own house—precluding the prolonged process, as it was in those days, of undressing completely.

He adds the next morning: 'Up with my mind disturbed and with my last night's doubts upon me, for which I deserve to be beaten if not really served as I am fearful of being, especially since God knows that I do not find honesty enough in my own mind but that upon a small temptation I could be false to her' (Mary Ashwell was still in his mind, evidently) 'and therefore ought not to expect more justice from her . . . After dinner comes Pembleton and I being out of humour would not see him, pretending business, but, Lord! with what jealousy did I walk up and down my chamber, listening to hear whether they danced or no, which they did.'

Mary Ashwell, an excellent dancer herself, was with master and pupil on that occasion, and eventually Sam went up and joined them. He could not keep away from either of the two women, though from different motives in each case. He ended, so far as Elizabeth was concerned, 'by resolving to prevent matters for the time to come as much as I can, it being to no purpose to trouble myself for what is past . . .' It was a somewhat rueful conclusion, but one to which even the most suspicious husbands were often forced in the seventeenth century.

Pembleton, however, was so assiduous and Mary Ashwell and Mrs. Pepys both so pleased with him, that the comic situation arose—worthy of Molière, Wycherley or Congreve—of Mr. Pepys himself taking dancing lessons to keep an eye on his temperamental spouse. 'I cannot,' he complains later in the month, 'get my mind to business as it should be and used to be before this dancing.' It was really wearing him out, though the others seemed to stand the strain without turning a hair. Yet, with characteristic self-discipline, he actually decided to fine himself half a crown every time his jealousy boiled over, consoling himself with the reflection that the lessons would only be going on for another month.

But meanwhile other things were happening too, and in Mr. Pepys' opinion were going from bad to worse. 'By many circumstances I am led to conclude that there is something more than ordinary between my wife and him, which do so trouble me that I know not at this very minute that I now write this almost what either I write or am doing nor how to carry myself to my wife in it, being unwilling to speak of it to her for making of any breach and other inconveniences nor let it pass for fear of her continuing to offend me . . .'

Mr. Pembleton was very polite, as became a dancing-master. On one occasion when Pepys came home and found him alone with Elizabeth, the astute fellow loudly declared that he could not possibly stay, as Miss Ashwell was not present to act as chaperone. But 'Lord!' writes the Diarist, 'to see how my jealousy wrought so far that I went softly up to see whether any of the beds were out of order or no, which I found not, but that did not content me . . .' He spent the rest of the evening pacing his chamber in moody silence, refusing to speak to his wife, 'being in a great doubt what to do'.

Next morning 'so I waked by 3 o'clock, my mind being troubled, and so took occasion by making water to wake my wife, and after having lain till past 4 o'clock seemed going to rise, though I did it only to see what she would do, and so going out of the bed she took hold of me and would know what ailed me and after many kind and some cross words I began to tax her discretion in yesterday's business, but she quickly told me my own, knowing well enough that it was my old disease of jealousy, which I denied, but to no purpose. After an hour's discourse, sometimes high and sometimes kind, I found very good reason to think that her freedom with him is very great and more than was convenient, but with no evil intent, and so after a while I caressed her and parted seeming friends, but she crying in a great discontent.'

At last 'my wife paid him off for this month also and so he is cleared. After dancing we took him down to supper and were very merry and I made myself so and kind to him as much as I could, to prevent his discourse, though I perceive to my trouble that he knows all and may do me the disgrace to publish it as much as he can. Which I take very ill and if too much provoked shall witness it to her.' Mr. Pembleton took his departure with due ceremony. But that was by no means the last of him.

3

Roving Eyes

SAM relieved his mind by resuming his old habit of
theatre-going which, as it usually did, turned his thoughts
once more to less innocent pleasures. 'So home,' he
writes on 29th May, 'and in my way did take two turns
forwards and backwards through the Fleete Ally to see a
couple of pretty strumpets that stood off the doors there and
God forgive me I could scarce stay myself from going into
their houses with them, so apt is my nature to evil after once,
as I have these two days, set upon pleasure again'.

A coolness now returned between husband and wife, the
latter again complaining of Sam's attentions to Mary Ashwell
and the former suspecting that Elizabeth was sending messages
to Pembleton by their man, or rather boy, servant. Mr. Pepys
watched his wife carefully when she dressed in the morning
to see if she put on 'drawers'. But even when she did, he could
not lull his suspicions. And sure enough—

'Presently after my coming home comes Pembleton, whether
by appointment or no I know not . . . but I took no notice of,
let them go up and Ashwell with them to dance, which they
did and I staid below in my chamber, but, Lord! how I listened
and laid my ear to the door and how I was troubled when I
heard them stand still and not dance.' But after a while the
dancing-master left, urbane as ever, and Pepys said nothing to
anyone about his renewed uneasiness. In any case, arrangements were being made for Mrs. Pepys to go on a visit to his
father in the country, and on 15th June she duly left, taking
Mary Ashwell with her.

Samuel, at a loose end, was soon in touch with his old friend

Betty Lane once more. Meeting her at Westminster Hall on
the 29th 'after great talk that she never went abroad with any
man as she used heretofore to do, I with one word got her to
go with me and to meet me at the further Rhenish wine house,
where I did give her a Lobster and do so touse her and feel her
all over, making her believe how fair and good a skin she has
and indeed she has a very white thigh and leg, but mon-
strous fat. When weary I did give over and somebody, having
seen some of our dalliance' (they were in a private room of
course, but the window gave on to the street) 'called aloud in
the street, "Sir! Why do you kiss the gentlewoman so?" and
flung a stone at the window, which vexed me, but I believe
they could not see my touzing her, and so we broke up and I
went out the back way, without being observed, I think.'
He adds, a little further on, 'I have used of late, since my wife
went, to make a bad use of my fancy with whatever woman I
have a mind to' (probably pretending she was Lady Castlemaine
or some other Court beauty) 'which I am ashamed of and shall
endeavour to do so no more.' The sentence sounds somewhat
hypocritical, but is highly typical of Sam. His 'endeavour' came
to very little, as we shall see in a moment.

On 9th July, in a 'little alehouse at Blackfriars . . . I kissed
three or four times the maid of the house, who is a pretty girl,
but very modest, and, God forgive me, had a mind to something more'. This was not the first time, nor the last, that
Mr. Pepys found an alehouse girl to be 'modest'. The surface
meaning of these statements is so unlikely, in seventeenth
century conditions, that one is driven to the conclusion either
that Sam's prickly conscience—for he certainly had one—was
really giving him trouble on these occasions, or that the girl,
for reasons of her own, probably financial, was simply playing
the prude with him.

On the very same day the Diarist had to ask God to forgive
him again. 'Thence I by water to Deptford and there mustered
the Yard, purposely, God forgive me, to find out Bagwell, a
carpenter, whose wife is a pretty woman, that I might have
some occasion of knowing him and forcing her to come to the

office again, which I did so luckily that going thence he and his wife did of themselves meet me in the way to thank me for my old kindness, but I spoke little to her, but shall give occasion for her coming to me.' There is no doubt, by this time, that Sam was getting a little exhilarated in his wife's absence and behaving like a regular Cavalier.

Less than a week later he was in Westminster Hall again, looking for Betty Lane 'and, God forgive me, had a mind to have got Mrs. Lane abroad' (i.e. to a tavern) 'or fallen in with any woman else (in that hot humour). But it so happened that she could not go out, nor I meet with anybody else and so I walked homeward, thanking God that I did not fall into any company to occasion spending time and money. To supper and then to a little viall' (i.e. playing on the viol) 'and to bed, sporting in my fancy with the Queen.' Two nights before, incidentally, he had gone to sleep 'fancying myself to sport with Mrs. Stewart' (*la belle* Stuart, now said to be the King's mistress) 'with great pleasure.' It was certainly high time that Mrs. Pepys returned from the country.

Sam was at Westminster Hall again on the 18th, looking over the shop-girls, one of whom, a Miss Howlett, he thought he could 'love very well'. But 'by and by Mrs. Lane comes and my' (neck) 'bands not being done' (i.e. starched) 'she and I posted' (arranged an appointment) 'and met at the Crown in the Palace Yard, where we eat a chicken I sent for and drank and were mighty merry and I had my full liberty of towzing her and doing what I would, but the last thing of all . . .' It seems that Mrs., i.e. 'mistress', Lane had some objection to positive fornication with Samuel, though it is not clear what this objection was, unless she preferred a bachelor lover. For the Diarist goes on:

'But, Lord! to see what a mind she has to a husband and how she showed me her hands to tell her her fortune and every thing she asked ended always whom and when she was to marry . . . thence walked home, all in a sweat with my tumbling of her and walking and so a little supper and to bed, fearful of having taken cold.' But he had 'pleasant dreams' that night.

He haunted the Westminster Hall promenades fairly assiduously after this encounter, but it was not until some days later that 'by agreement we met at the Parliament stairs. In my way down to the boat who should meet us but my lady Jemimah' (daughter of the Earl of Sandwich and a friend of Mrs. Pepys) 'who saw me lead her but said nothing to me of her though I ought to speak to her to see whether she would take notice of it or no, and off to Stangate and so to the King's head at Mambeth march, and had variety of meats and drinks, but I did so towse her and handled her, but could get nothing more from her though I was very near it. But as wanton and bucksome as she is she dares not adventure upon the business.' As we have seen, Mistress Lane was on the look-out for a match less encumbered than Sam Pepys.

It was on 10th August that Mr. Pepys discovered that he was not the only member of the Tangier Commission to respond to the charms of young women moving in far less exalted circles. 'Hither came W. Howe about business,' he writes. Howe was the current Deputy Treasurer of the Navy, a musician like Sam himself and a fellow whom he rather liked, though later on, like so many other friends who seemed all right at one time, Howe turned out to be a rogue, and was arrested for theft. 'And he and I had a great deal of discourse about my Lord Sandwich and I find by him that my Lord do dote upon one of the daughters of Mrs. Becke, where he lies, so that he spends his time and money upon her.'

Sandwich had fallen ill in April, and had gone down to what was then the quiet country village of Chelsea to recuperate. He had been staying there off and on throughout the summer (his wife and family being at his country estate) in the modest home of a retired London merchant named Becke. Samuel had paid his patron several visits there, and duly noted that the merchant's daughter Betty had what it takes to attract a connoisseur.

'He tells me,' the Diarist goes on, referring to Howe, 'she' (i.e. Betty Becke) 'is a woman of a very bad fame and very imprudent and' (Howe) 'has told my Lord so, yet for all that my Lord do spend all his evenings with her, though he be at Court in the day time and that the world do take notice of it, and that Pickering' (a foppish courtier and bad violin player, who hung round Lord Sandwich) 'is only there as a blind, that the world may think that my lord spends his time with him when he do worse and that hence it is that my Lord has no more mind to go into the country' (to his estate) 'than he has. In fine, I perceive my Lord is dabbling with this wench, for which I am sorry, though I do not wonder at it, being a man amorous enough, and now begins to allow himself the liberty that he says every body else at Court takes.'

This pompous sermon might have been uttered by Lord Sandwich's grandfather instead of by the hero of a hundred 'amours' with young ladies just like Betty Becke, whom he had, moreover, thoroughly approved of up to that date. However, Howe's news had gravely disturbed the vigilant cousin of the earl. What would happen to the Clerk of the Acts and Tangier Commissioner if Sandwich created a scandal? A liaison with a Court lady would not have been so bad. But a merchant's daughter! If the tale were true, something ought to be done about it. But perhaps it was all only the usual Whitehall malicious gossip. Sandwich certainly had plenty of enemies, as his cousin was already uncomfortably aware.

On 12th August Mrs. Pepys returned from the country, where she had managed to quarrel with both Mary Ashwell and Sam's father. The Diarist of course stood up for both Mary, who defended herself with great eloquence, and his parent. He had a long private talk with his admired Ashwell—though out of doors, accompanying her on a visit to her father's house—and found to his amazement that Elizabeth had told her that it was he who wanted to get rid this accomplished companion. But Miss Ashwell informed the distracted husband that in her opinion Elizabeth would prefer a companion less likely than the virtuous speaker to give a wife's little games away.

And sure enough, to Sam's horror and disgust, a day or two later the egregious Mr. Pembleton called, all smiles, to enquire whether the dancing lessons were to be renewed. The Diarist sent him off with a flea in his ear, 'I think without any time of receiving any great satisfaction from my wife or invitation to come again'. Miss Ashwell duly left on 25th August, but Mrs. Pepys did not seem, after all, to be very glad of it, and taxed Sam with deliberate plotting to keep her from 'pleasure', 'which,' the Diarist confesses, 'though I am sorry to see she minds it, is true enough in a great degree'. So he put her in a better temper by taking her off into the country again for a few days.

At Whitehall on the 17th, a Mr. Moore, an intimate friend of the Sandwich family, told Samuel that his patron had in fact been dangerously indiscreet. Moore 'tells me with great sorrow of my Lord's being debauched he fears by this woman at Chelsey, which I am troubled at and resolve to speak to him of it if I can seasonably'. The tale was already being related with glee by Sandwich's opponents at Court, and heard with something like dread by those who were dependent on him. The earl seemed to have become really infatuated with Betty Becke. It was no passing caprice, and the girl was said to be a 'common strumpet'.

Samuel became terribly uneasy. He was on the point of raising the subject with his touchy patron when he heard from Ned Pickering that on the latter's merely pulling a long face, without uttering a word, when the earl had praised Betty Becke in his presence, Sandwich had sent him to the kitchen. 'So I am resolved not to meddle with it,' writes Sam on 7th September.

He elaborates this decision a couple of days later, after another talk with the 'coxcomb' Pickering. 'He telling me the whole business of my Lord's folly with this Mrs. Becke at Chelsey, of all which I am ashamed to see my Lord so grossly play the beast and fool, to the flinging off of all honour, friends, servants and every thing and person that is good, and will only have his private lust undisturbed with this common . . .' here the Diarist's frantic anxiety about his prospects gets the better of him, and he gives vent to an unprintable obscenity—'his sitting up night after night alone, suffering nobody to come to them, and all the day too, casting off Pickering, basely reproaching him with his small estate, which yet is a good one, and other poor courses to obtain privacy beneath his honour, and with his carrying her abroad and playing on his lute under her window, and forty other poor sordid things, which I am grieved to hear; but believe it to no purpose for me to meddle with it, but let him go on till God Almighty and his own conscience and thoughts of his lady and family do it.'

Distracted by this very serious threat to his fortunes, Mr. Pepys bethought himself of that other Betty, Mrs. Lane. A first visit to Westminster Hall drew a blank, but next day 'in the afternoon, telling my wife that I go to Deptford, I went by water to Westminster Hall and there finding Mrs. Lane took her over to Lambeth, where we were lately and there did what I would with her, but only the main thing, which she would not consent to'. One may wonder at Sam's patience with this obstinate young woman. Though he would have been glad enough to make her his mistress if she had been agreeable to any such thing, he was rather relieved, in fact well enough content, to find that she had other views; a permanent liaison might have eventually caused trouble with his only too jealous wife, and he was the kind of amorist who prefers a half-way house 'to his mind' to the potentially burdensome responsibilities of a full-scale intrigue which might turn out to be a nuisance in the end. In spite of Betty Lane's over-fat legs, she greatly attracted him physically, and the 'towsing and tumbling' satisfied him well enough for the time being.

In November, refreshed by this encounter, Samuel changed his mind again about speaking to Lord Sandwich. 'Mr. Moore and I discoursing of my Lord's negligence in attendance at Court and the discourse the world makes of it, with the too great reason that I believe there is for it; I resolved and took coach to his lodgings, thinking to speak with my Lord about it without more ado. Here I met Mr. Howe and he and I largely about it and he very soberly acquainted me how things are with my Lord, that my Lord do not do anything like himself but follows his folly and spends his time either at cards at Court with the ladies when he is there at all or else at Chelsey with the slut to his great disgrace and indeed I do see and believe that my Lord do apprehend that he do grow less too at Court. Anon my Lord do come in and I begun to fall in discourse with him, but my heart did misgive me that my Lord would not take it well and then found him not in a humour to talk and so after a few ordinary words, my Lord not talking in the manner as he uses to do, I took leave and spent some time with W. Howe again and told him how I could not do what I had so great a mind and resolution to do, but that I thought it would be as well to do it in writing, which he approves of and so I took leave of him and by coach home, my mind being full of it and in pain concerning it.'

On 17th November, accordingly, he wrote a long letter to Sandwich. On the 22nd he called to see how the earl was taking it. Sandwich asked him who were gossiping, and Samuel named Dr. Pierce, Ned Pickering and one or two others, but not Moore or Howe. The peer told him quietly that the Beckes were decent people, and that he meant to live as he pleased. Then he changed the subject, beginning to talk about pictures. For some time after this his attitude to his cousin remained cold. The intrigue with Betty Becke continued; Sam was on tenterhooks for a while, but then the wind seemed to change. When Mr. Pepys begged respectfully for the loan of the earl's coach and six to attend the funeral of his cousin Edward, the request was granted. Samuel breathed again. He had taken a great risk, but it looked as though he had weathered the storm. Time would show.

And now that this tricky affair was over, there was time for girls again. After all, one wife and one pretty constant girl-friend were nothing like enough for this industrious Civil Servant. The harder he worked, the more he found he wanted to ring the changes. On the evening of 12th December, after a prolonged session over accounts at the office 'I spent a little time . . . walking in the garden and in the mean time while I was walking Mrs. Pen's pretty maid' (on whom Sam had had his eye for some considerable time) 'came by my side and went into the office, but finding nobody there I went in to her, being glad of the occasion. She told me as she was going out again that there was nobody there and that she came for a sheet of paper. So I told her I would supply her and left her in the office and went into my office and opened my garden door thinking to have got her in and there to have caressed her and, seeming looking for paper, I told her this way was as near a way for her, but she told me she had left the door open and so did not come to me. So I carried her some paper and kissed her, leading her by the hand to the garden door and there let her go.'

The girl clearly knew what he was after, and did not choose that he should get it, probably because of the close connection of the Penn family with his. Mr. Pepys was disconcerted. 'But, Lord!' he continues, 'to see how much I was put out of order by this surprisal and how much I could have subjected my mind to have treated and been found with this wench and how afterwards I was troubled to think what if she should tell this and whether I had spoke or done any thing that might be unfit for her to tell. But I think there was nothing more passed than just what I here write.' No one would think anything of Penn's maid reporting a kiss snatched by her master's friend. Neither would she herself dream of reporting, still less complaining of, any such triviality in the circumstances of those days. Yet it is rather significant that Pepys had already forgotten whether he did anything more than kiss her. One can hardly fail to deduce that the great Diary is by no means complete in its accounts of sexual adventures, and hence that in such cases Sam is not always to be given the benefit of the doubt by moralists.

The year 1664 opened with a great event in the Diarist's love-life. On the afternoon of Saturday, 16th January, Mrs. Betty Lane at last conceded 'the main thing'. No details are available in print. But it is now that Samuel begins occasionally to write even his cipher in a foreign language. The natural inference is that his amours were becoming more serious and complicated. At any rate, that night his mind was '*un peu* troubled *pour ce que fait* to-day'. He wrote this dog-French, too, in a different cipher from that which he generally used.

The odd thing was that this erotic success made him more jealous of Mrs. Pepys than ever. Catching sight of Pembleton in church that Sunday—for our Diarist never missed a sermon—he was positively unable to eat any supper in the evening. Without going into any technical subtleties of psycho-analysis, we may assume that his own lapse brought the possibility of similar transgressions by his wife more to the fore of that restless 'mind' of his. He even wondered, on returning from the office on the Monday, what Wayneman, his manservant, was doing alone with Mrs. Pepys.

It is much more readily understandable that with his senses now alerted by the successful intrigue with Betty Lane, he took a morbid interest in a somewhat sordid scene that took place in the City late on the night of 3rd February. 'This night, late coming in my coach, coming up Ludgate Hill, I saw two gallants and their footmen taking a pretty wench, which I have much eyed, lately set up shop upon the hill, a seller of riband and gloves. They seek to drag her by some force, but the wench went and I believe had her turn served, but, God forgive me! what thoughts and wishes I had of being in their place.'

On the whole, contemporary evidence gives the shop-girls of seventeenth century London a character both gay and shrewd, not unlike the *midinettes* of nineteenth century Paris, though perhaps even more 'knowing'. With few resources but their own wits in a world of ruthlessly predatory males, they had all the dice loaded against them in a way almost impossible for their modern counterparts to realise, since today the circumstances are just the other way about. The pursuit of the girl from Harridges, even in force and with up-to-date equipment, has become as dangerous as hunting a buffalo, and no doubt that it is exactly what it ought to be; but in 1664 the boot was on the other foot. The young woman who sold gloves on Ludgate Hill or 'bands' in Westminster Hall had to defend herself without benefit of society, for society, so far from 'spoiling' her like a vestal virgin, which is the mode of the nineteen-fifties, was already inclined to regard her as in any case a bit of a whore. She often was, but not always. She almost invariably began, like any other girl, by playing for a safe marriage, and she generally got it in the end, though sometimes it had to be *via* a series of rich protectors.

In any case, Mr. Pepys would have been quite at a loss to know what to do with his spare time in twentieth-century London for his means, even now, were limited. He could not go in for wholeheartedly fashionable merrymaking. So without the gay sales-ladies of the shops, so easy of access, he would have felt like an anchorite.

The day after the scene on Ludgate Hill he called 'at my little milliner's, where I chatted with her, her husband out of the way, and a mad merry slut she is'. He did not go on to Westminster Hall on this occasion, but went home to hear his wife's account of the funeral of a deceased friend at Wapping. This was by no means a wholly gloomy story, for it included the anecdote of 'how her mayd Jane going into the boat did fall down and show her arse in the boat'. The farcical and the sad, as always, were never far apart in those days.

At this period, Sam was doing his best to get Betty Lane married. He was nervous of so close an association as the present with a spinster who might later on prove dangerous, whereas he anticipated perfectly smooth sailing in an intrigue with someone else's wife, which was the general form of love-affair among his contemporaries. In this connection he 'seriously advised' Mr. 'Hawly,' who has already been mentioned, and 'inquired his condition', i.e. his financial status, just like a parent or a matrimonial agent. However, Hawly escaped this trap for the time being.

Mr. Pepys was annoyed at his failure, and began to be cool with Mrs. Betty. He still took her out. But 'I went also out of the Hall with Mrs. Lane to the Swan at Mrs. Herbert's in the Palace Yard to try a couple of bands and did (though I had a mind to be playing the fool with her) purposely stay but a little while and kept the door open and called the master and mistress of the house one after another to drink and talk with

me and showed them both my old and new bands. So that as
I did nothing so they are able to bear witness that I had no
opportunity there to do anything.' This extreme prudence is
not accounted for in the Diary. Either Sam was beginning to
be terrified of his wife—they had had many quarrels lately—or
else his mistress, the other Betty, was herself terrifying him in
some way, perhaps by veiled hints of blackmail.

On 11th May Samuel's jealousy of Mrs. Pepys received a jolt
from a direction he had never dreamed of. His uncle Wight,
from whom they had expectations and who did not get on
with his own wife, a lady described by Sam as 'pettish' and
'ugly', actually suggested to Elizabeth Pepys, 'after discourse
of her want of children and his also', 'how he thought it
would be best for him and her to have one between them and
he would give her £500 either in money or jewels beforehand
and make the child his heir. He commended her body and
discoursed that for all he knew the thing was lawful. She says
she did give him a very warm answer, such as he did not excuse
himself by saying that he said this in jest, but told her that
since he saw what her mind was he would say no more to her
of it and desired her to make no words of it. It seemed he did
say all this in a kind of counterfeit laugh, but by all words that
passed, which I cannot now so well set down, it is plain to me
that he was in good earnest and that I fear all his kindness is
but only his lust to her. What to think of it of a sudden I know
not but I think not to take notice yet of it to him till I have
thought better of it.'

The situation was awkward, for neither he nor Elizabeth
wished to offend the wealthy old rascal, but this remarkable
story must have made the Diarist reflect that whatever Mrs.
Pepys might think of young men like Pembleton and their
ex-manservant Wayneman, a riotous lad now on his way to the
West Indies, she was at least not the whore he had once, in a
fit of temper, called her. The expression, of course, meant no
more than our 'bitch' in the language of the time, but it had
been strong enough to make her cry and the Diarist to repent
and apologise. They both desired children, but the health of

both was poor in a sense that may have some significance in this connection. Ever since Sam's operation for calculus of the kidney he had experienced intermittent pain in urinating, obstinate constipation and swelling of the testicles. The trouble may conceivably have affected his generative capacity. Mrs. Pepys, too, suffered from internal abscesses and bleeding, being often confined to bed for days on this account. These conditions may or may not be compatible with fertility in either partner, but on the face of it they do not seem very favourable to the founding of a family. No doubt Elizabeth's childlessness had much to do with her frequent outbursts of temper, and it is all the more to her credit that she declined Uncle Wight's not wholly disinterested proposition.

All through this spring and summer there had been rumours of war with the Dutch, who were beginning to challenge English command of the seas, especially off West Africa, in the East and in the West Indies. Colonial Holland was strongest in the Malay Archipelago, the Gulf of Guinea settlements and Guiana. Spices, slaves and silk came from these places. The two great mercantile nations of the north had already fallen out in Cromwell's time over the East Indies trade, and also about the North Sea fisheries. Blake had eventually got the better of Tromp in the quarrel, and the great Dutch admiral had been killed. By the late fifties Dutch expansion in the Far East had been decisively checked.

In the early sixties the area of dispute shifted to West Africa, where the English were determined to hold the lion's share of the lucrative slave trade. As early as October 1663 British men-of-war were raiding the Dutch coastal posts, and on 8th September 1664 the settlement in North America known as New Netherlands or New Amsterdam was seized by Colonel Nicholl and renamed New York after King Charles' brother, the Lord High Admiral. Mr. Pepys would have given this item of news a little more space in his journal if he had guessed even remotely at the momentous consequences for the whole world that were to ensue from this piratical performance.

By way of reprisal, Admiral de Ruyter recaptured the

African ports and attacked the British colony of Barbados, but as yet there was no official declaration of war. Parliament was holding back for a reason which Samuel knew very well. The Navy Office, through no fault of his, but on account of the jealousies between the other principal officers, was not functioning well. Despite the fury of the City and the anxiety of the Duke of York to distinguish himself at sea, the House would not vote the necessary funds for war until the Navy had been put on a proper war footing.

Mr. Pepys' hands were again full with contractual and supply business. For weeks he had no time at all for 'bucksome' Mrs. Betty Lane and little for the fretful Elizabeth. The Secretary-Registrar at the Navy Office was beginning to be one of the busiest—because he was one of the most conscientious—men in the country. To such heights of dignity had the poor tailor's son risen in the last few years. By the end of 1664 he was worth £1,349, more than £500 more than in the previous year. He was spending plentifully on servants now, paying the cost of their liveries, extra food and entertainment in addition to their wages. On the other hand, Tangier was bringing him in £300 a year and there were other perquisites, which looked like increasing.

The Dutch trouble had two further important results for Sam. Lord Sandwich took a protective fleet to sea, and an extra commissioner was appointed to the Navy Board in the person of Viscount Brouncker. The Viscount had been the first President of the Royal Society. He was a good mathematician, and one of those people whom the Secretary liked at first and detested afterwards. The time was to come when he was to call Brouncker 'rotten-hearted' and 'false' and to find his vulgar mistress a nuisance; but Brouncker, with all his faults, was an able fellow and really an asset to the Navy Office.

These calls upon Mr. Pepys' time did not turn him into a Puritan; far from it. But for a while he did rather neglect his 'cods', as he called them.

4

Rake's Calendar

ON 11th July 1664 Mrs. Pepys left for her annual holiday in the country, Sam riding with her as far as Barnet. As usual, he was not long in consoling himself for her absence. This time it was on a visit to his barber's, 'to have my Periwigg he lately made me cleansed of its nits', that Mr. Pepys spotted the barber's maid Jane. 'I talked with her and sending her of an errand to Dr. Clerk's did meet her and took her into a little alehouse in Brewers' Yard and there did sport with her, without any knowledge of her though, and a very pretty innocent girl she is.' He evidently expected more than 'sport', but with characteristic good humour—he was good-tempered with all women except his wife and Betty Lane—turned his disappointment into gratitude for the small mercies he in fact received. In the future he was fated to see quite a lot of this Jane (whose surname was Welsh) though a good deal less than he hoped.

Two days later came great news from the matrimonial market. Betty Lane had married at last. The husband was a man named Martin 'that serves Captain Marsh. She has gone abroad' (not to foreign parts, but only on some local jaunt or other) 'with him to-day, very fine. I must have a bout with her very shortly, to see how she finds marriage.' All's well that ends well, he might have thought. Now that he had a married mistress he could really let himself go. It was unfortunate for Betty, but not for Sam, that Mr. Martin did not prove to be at all an ideal husband.

Mr. Pepys was in such a hurry to take advantage of his new-found status that the very next day he paid a visit of congratulation to the couple's lodgings. Mr. Martin, as it happened, was out, and his newly wedded wife 'there suffered me to deal with her as I hoped to do and by and by her husband comes, a sorry, simple fellow, and his letter to her which she proudly showed me a simple, nonsensical thing. A man of no discourse and I fear married her to make a prize of, which he is mistaken in and a sad wife I believe she will prove to him, for she urged me to appoint a time as soon as he is gone out of town to give her a meeting next week.' It seemed, for the moment, an ideal situation, if not an ideal husband. But before long Mr. Martin's very idiocy was going to cause trouble between the lovers.

Not just yet, however. On the 23rd, 'being in an idle, wanton humour, walked through Fleet Alley and there stood a most pretty wench at one of the doors, so I took a turn or two, but what by sense of honour and conscience I would not go in, but much against my will took coach and away, and away to Westminster Hall and there by light of Mrs. Lane and plotted with her to go over the water' (of the Thames, of course). 'So met at White's stairs in Chanel Row and over to the old house at Lambeth Marsh and there eat and drank and had my pleasure of her twice, she being the strangest woman in talk of love to her husband sometimes and sometimes again she do not care for him, and yet willing enough to allow me a liberty of doing what I would with her. So spending 5s. or 6s. upon her I could do what I would and after an hour's stay and more back again and set her ashore there again.'

But even this orgy was not enough for the Diarist. Thoroughly aroused by his recent experiences 'I forward to Fleet Street and called at Fleet Alley, not knowing how to command myself, and went in and there saw what formerly I have been acquainted with, the wickedness of these houses and the forcing a man to present expense. The woman indeed is a most lovely woman, but I had no courage to meddle with her for fear of her not being wholesome' (syphilis was of course rampant in such places) 'and so counterfeiting that I had not money enough, it was pretty to see how cunning she was, would not suffer me to have to do in any manner with her after she saw I had no money, but told me then I would not come again, but she now was sure I would come again, but I hope in God I shall not, for though she be one of the prettiest women I ever saw, yet I fear her abusing me' (i.e. infecting him with venereal disease). 'So, desiring God to forgive me this vanity, I went home . . . weary of the pleasure I have had to-day and ashamed to think of it.' Samuel was a very straightforward case of sex obsession, after all. He lusted after every 'pretty' woman he caught a glimpse of, but was remarkably often satisfied with just taking another look at her.

It was during Mrs. Pepys' annual summer holiday that the Diarist's mind most often suffered from such visions. 'Do what I could,' he writes on 25th July 1664, 'I could not keep myself from going through Fleet Lane, but had the sense of safety and honour not to go in and the rather being a holiday I feared I might meet with some people that might know me . . . I walked all round that end of the town among the loathsome people and houses but, God be thanked, had no desire to visit any of them.' It was, of course, an experience common among young men in his condition. The legitimate partner being away, potential illegitimate companions are considered and preferably such as the investigator is unlikely to come across later. Pepys knew plenty of the wives and daughters of his friends, and greatly admired some of them, but with a very jealous wife in the offing he was too prudent, as a rule, to embark on intrigues with members of his own circle. Consequently the prostitutes had a look in—but only a look, for in the seventeenth century they were in general distinctly inferior to those of the following age, which was on the whole more scientific and less romantic in the field of erotics than its predecessor. The typical eighteenth-century male regarded the sexual act rather as a biological necessity, best cultivated with professionals, than as an adventure to be pursued with amateurs. Accordingly, supply rose in quality and quantity to meet demand. But in Samuel's day, as in our own, out and out professional whores were generally despised, and consequently most of them, however youthful, were physical wrecks.

In that frank society, however, again as in our own, a great deal of satisfaction could be obtained, by those who had a mind to it, in mere talk. Next day, at a dinner party in the house of a cousin, one Anthony Joyce, 'very merry we were and when the women were merry and rose from table, I above with them, ne'er a man but I. I began discourse of my not getting of children and prayed them to give me their opinions and advice and they freely and merrily did give me these ten among them. (1) Do not hug my wife too hard nor too much (2) eat no late suppers (3) drink juyce of sage (4) tent and toast (5) wear cool holland drawers (6) keep stomach warm and back cool (7) upon query whether it was best to do at night or morn, they answered me neither one nor other, but when we had most mind to it (8) wife not to go too straight-laced (9) myself to drink mum' (a kind of ale) 'and sugar (10) Mrs. Ward did give me, to change my place' (i.e. in the matrimonial bed).

'The 3rd, 4th, 6th, 7th and 10th they all did seriously declare and lay much stress upon them as rules fit to be observed indeed and especially the last, to lie with our heads where our heels do or at least to make the bed high at feet and low at head.'

It must have been a hilarious party, though to the gentleman not much more than a slight palliative to his sexual pre-occupations. He might have consulted Ovid's *Ars Amatoria* with advantage, but probably cold print appealed to him less than personal exchanges. In desperation he returned to the harlots. 'It raining, turned into Fleet Alley and there was with Cocke an hour or so. The jade, whether I would not give her money or not enough, she would not offer to invite to do anything, but on the contrary saying she had no time, which I was glad of, for I had no mind to meddle with her, but had my end to see what a cunning jade she was, to see her impudent tricks and ways of getting money and raising the reckoning by still calling for things, that it come to 6 or 7 shillings presently. So away home, glad I escaped without any inconvenience.'

He really could not bear these creatures, forlorn though he felt himself to be. It was a great relief when Mrs. Pepys returned from the country early in August.

On the 15th he ran into Mrs. Lane at the Trumpet Inn near Westminster Hall. She told him 'a sad story how her husband, as I feared, proves not worth a farthing and that she is with child and undone if I do not get him a place. I had my pleasure here of her and she, like an impudent jade, depends upon my kindness to her husband, but I will have no more to do with her, let her brew as she has baked, seeing she would not take my counsel about Hawly' (a more suitable prospective cuckold whom Sam, as already mentioned, had chosen for her). The Diarist's relations with this ex-shopgirl continued throughout the ten years covered by his journal. Though she often exasperated him and he was too intelligent not to know her for what she was, an extremely mercenary, immoral and shallow young woman, he could not keep away from her, even when Mrs. Pepys was in town.

About this time he began to pursue a similar course with Jane Welsh, his barber's maid, on whom he had long had his eye. 'I got the poor wretch to promise to meet me in the Abbey on to-morrow come sennight, telling me that her master and mistress have a mind to get her a husband and so will not let her go abroad without them, but only in sermon time on Sundays she do go out. I would I could get a good husband for her, for she is one I always thought a good-natured as well as a well-looked girl.' The idea was, of course, as so often in those days and later, to turn a prospective mistress of inferior social rank, into a married woman—when, paradoxically enough, it would be easier to carry on an intrigue with her—and thus earn her eternal gratitude and fidelity. The domestic servants and shopgirls who were the objects of these interested attentions by gentlemen were as a rule ready enough to fall in with the plan, for while they remained single their economic dependence rendered them practically prisoners, with no ultimate prospect but that of prostitution. At the same time, Sam was at the same game with Mrs. Bagwell, the pretty wife of the Deptford dockyard carpenter already mentioned, with the variant of 'getting her husband a place' (i.e. promotion) 'which I will do'. Both these affairs started slowly. Jane Welsh, in particular, proved very disappointing.

On the other hand Mrs. Bagwell, who had made a great show of reluctance and modesty at first, yielded on 15th November. 'Bagwell's wife with much ado followed me through Moorfields to a blind alehouse and there I did caress her and eat and drink and many hard looks and sooth the poor wretch did give me and I think verily was troubled at what I did, but at last after many protestings by degrees I did arrive at what I would, with great pleasure.'

By this time, unofficial war with the Dutch was going on, so that there were plenty of jobs to be had in the Navy, even for wastrels. Martin, Betty 'Lane's' husband—Sam's romance with her might almost be called 'My Eye and Betty Martin' in nineteenth-century slang—joined the Fleet at Portsmouth as a purser. On 6th December 1664 'I to Westminster Hall and there spent much time till towards noon to and fro with people. So by and by Mrs. Lane comes and plucks me by the cloak to speak to me, and I was fain to go to her shop, and pretending to buy some bands made her go home and by and by followed her and there did what I would with her and so after many discourses and her intreating me to do something for her husband, which I promised to do, and buying a little band of her, which I intend to keep to, I took leave, there coming a couple of footboys to her with a coach to fetch her abroad, I know not to whom. She is great with child and says I must be godfather, but I do not intend it.' It is pretty certain that Betty was not entirely dependent on the Diarist's good offices, but that did not seem to worry him at all. Jealousy clearly played no part in his affair with her.

A day or two later 'find I cannot prevail with Jane' (the barber's maid) 'to go forth with me, but though I took a good occasion of going to the Trumpet she declined coming, which vexed me'. He adds in his dog-French: '*Je avait grande envie envers elle avec vrai amour et passion.*' Like other highly susceptible gentlemen, Mr. Pepys, when rebuffed, fancied himself harder hit than he really was.

The Bagwell intrigue, however, was going strong at this time. On 19th December, on which day Sam, in a dispute with his wife about the servants, gave poor Elizabeth a black eye, 'not finding Bagwell's wife as I expected, I to the 'Change and there walked up and down, and then home, and she being come I bid her go and stay at Mooregate for me and after going up to my wife (whose eye is very bad but she is in very good temper to me) and after dinner I to the place and walked round the fields again and again but not finding her I to the 'change and there found her waiting for me and took her away and to an alehouse and there made I much of her and then away thence and to another and endeavoured to caress her but *elle ne voulait pas*, which did vex me, but I think it was chiefly not having a good easy place to do it upon'.

That night 'to bed, my mind, God forgive me, too much running upon what I can *ferais avec la femme de Bagwell demain*, having promised to go to Deptford and *a aller a sa maison avec son mari* when I come thither.

'20th. Up and walked to Deptford where after doing something at the Yard I walked without being observed with Bagwell home to his house . . . after dinner I found occasion of sending him abroad and then alone *avec elle je tentais a faire ce que je voudrais et contre sa force je le faisais bien que passe a mon contentment.*' In other words, the important guest at this humble home, after dismissing his anxious host, fell upon the latter's wife with such importunity that in spite of her natural reluctance to act the whore in her husband's own house she capitulated, much to the Diarist's 'satisfaction', as he complacently records in the French he was beginning to find superior to English in the description of these fortunate occasions.

In such relatively few passages of Samuel's journal the author appears as a bit of a rogue. But in far more he comes out as a rather exceptionally good-hearted and quite intelligent man, with only a few amusing foibles. The sentiments and manners of the seventeenth century in England regarded such behaviour as that of the Clerk of the Acts to the hospitable carpenter and his wife as a negligible peccadillo. Indeed, it is very likely that in view of those same sentiments and manners, the carpenter himself would not have seriously objected to, and would even perhaps have encouraged, his wife's adultery with so benevolent a patron—perhaps he did actually do so. That would be no excuse in the opinion of a theoretical moralist in that age, as in this. Such a moralist would condemn everyone concerned, but practical citizens did not do so in 1664. Moral indignation in sexual matters was not an emotion often indulged in by the ordinary Londoner until a hundred years later, when sensibility became the mode.

The year 1665 started auspiciously for the amorous inclinations of Mr. Pepys. On 2nd January 'I to my barber's . . . and there had a little opportunity of speaking with my Jane alone and did give her something and of herself she did tell me a place where I might come to her on Sunday next, which I will not fail . . . thence to the Swan and there did sport a good while with Herbert's' (the landlady's) 'young kinswoman without hurt, though they being abroad, the old people. Then to the Hall' (i.e. Westminster Hall) 'and there agreed with Mrs. Martin' (so called by Sam for the first time) 'and to her lodgings which she has now taken to lie in . . . here I did *ce que je voudrais avec* her most freely and it having cost 2s. in wine and cake upon her I away sick of her impudence . . .'

It may be thought that the economical Diarist was a little hard on poor Betty, but he was by now rather a fine gentleman and no doubt her tactless begging did get on his nerves to some extent. He had already begun to express in other parts of his journal a certain distaste for low company, sometimes including that of his many poverty-stricken relatives; all the same, he could not give Betty Martin up, any more than he could give up the other Elizabeth, his wife, with whom he had nearly as many rows and reconciliations.

Jane Welsh did not keep the Sunday appointment. It turned out, first that she had a 'sweetheart' of her own rank in life, and secondly that she was 'undone', i.e. had made a fool of herself. 'She had made herself sure to a fellow that comes to their house that can only fiddle for his living, and did keep him company . . . she was sure to him never to leave him for anybody else . . . they were this day' (20th January) 'contriving to get her presently to marry one Hayes that was there and I did seem to persuade her to it. And at last got them' (the barber and his wife) 'to suffer me to advise privately and by that means had her company and think I shall meet her next Sunday, but I do really doubt she will be undone in marrying this fellow. But I did give her my advice and so let her do her pleasure, so I have now and then her company. Thence to the Swan at noon and there sent for a bit of meat and dined and had my *baiser* of the *fille* of the house there but nothing *plus*.' It was not much of a compensation for Jane's deceit, but better than nothing. No doubt it made Sam feel that after all he was as good a lady-killer as the best of them. In any case, it is evident that he had not yet despaired of Jane—quite the contrary, in fact.

Nevertheless, he failed on two subsequent occasions to get hold of Jane. So 'I away by coach to the 'change and thence home to dinner. And finding Mrs. Bagwell waiting at the office after dinner' (after all, her husband was a dockyard employee) 'away she and I to a cabaret where she and I have eat before and there I had her company *tout* and had *mon plaisir* of *elle*. But strange to see how a woman, notwithstanding her greatest pretences of love *a son mari* and religion may be *vaincue*.' This Anglo-French rigmarole shows Samuel in a rather unpleasantly fatuous light. It was far less his own prowess as a seducer than the lady's wish to help her husband that had 'conquered' Mrs. Bagwell. However, the illusion was perhaps natural in the circumstances, for probably the woman was no worse an actress than the rest of her sex.

The Diarist now makes a vow to '*laisser aller les femmes*' for no less than a whole month. But only three days later he had a heart to heart talk with Jane, during which there is some reason to suppose, from an obscene expression in the MS. of the journal, that a certain amount of sexual play, if nothing more, occurred. 'She is resolved to stick to this sweetheart of hers, one Harbing (a very sorry little fellow and poor) which I did in a word or two endeavour to dissuade her from . . . thence led her about down to the Three Cranes and there took boat for the Falcon and at a house looking into the fields there took up and sat an hour or two talking and discoursing . . . thence having endeavoured to make her think of making herself happy by staying out her time with her master and other counsels, but she told me she could not do it, for it was her fortune to have this man, though she did believe it would be to her ruine, which is a strange, stupid thing, to a fellow of no kind of worth in the world and a beggar to boot.'

The frequency with which really nice girls throw themselves away on hopeless loafers, not even good-looking, is nowadays accounted for by invoking the maternal instinct. This explanation had not occurred to Mr. Pepys. He could therefore only react to the situation with contemptuous impatience, if not anger. Like most of his contemporaries, he was certainly an extremely impatient person. British phlegm was not very conspicuous in those days, and Sam seldom exhibited it. He was also very persistent, but his persistence in this case did not find its reward. By April he is writing that 'Jane is quite undone, taking the idle fellow for her husband, yet not married, and lay with him several weeks that had another wife and child, and she is now going into Ireland.' That was the end of her originally strong attraction for Pepys. He did see her again, a year later, and had a drink with her, but nothing more.

Of course there were others. Even his cousin Mrs. Turner, a most respectable woman, wife of the Recorder of York and often at Court, who had two young sons, aroused a momentary kindling of Samuel's eternally smouldering lust. When he called on her one morning in February 'she was dressing herself by the fire in her chamber and there took occasion to show me her leg, which indeed is the finest I ever saw, and she not a little proud of it'. Luckily for all concerned this incident had no sequel. It is only interesting as a sidelight on the freedom of manners at the time, by no means confined to cousins.

Mrs. Bagwell remained his chief standby at this period. On 20th February he wrote 'a letter to my lord Sandwich for her husband's advance into a better ship as there should be occasion . . . by and by did go down by water to Deptford and then down further and so landed at the lower end of the town, and it being dark —' Here the Diarist relapses into his execrable French, to the effect that he entered the carpenter's house and had his will of the man's wife 'though with a great deal of difficulty', as before. Mrs. Bagwell evidently did not care for these domestic visits, and in fact shows very little sign throughout the affair of being as personally interested in Sam as he thought she was. In the amorous struggle on this occasion she twisted the forefinger of his left hand so badly that he had a 'mighty pain' in it the next morning.

As for Betty Martin, she was not accessible for the moment, being 'brought to bed of a boy and christened Charles, which I am very glad of, for I was fearful of being called to be a godfather to it. But it seems it was to be done suddenly and so I escaped. It is strange to see how a liberty and going abroad without purpose of doing anything do lead a man to what is bad for I was just upon going to her . . .' The last sentence, not very intelligible on the face of it, seems to mean that Sam, finding himself at Westminster for no particular reason—which may however be doubted, since the Hall was a great recruiting ground for ladies of easy virtue—had suddenly decided to look up Betty when he heard the news, and was thus saved from something 'bad', i.e. the breaking of his recent oath to have nothing more to do with her for a while. But he was soon on as intimate terms as ever with this old friend, her husband being 'gone away', as he writes, 'like a fool, into France'.

On 4th March 1665, war was formally proclaimed, at the Royal Exchange in London, against the United Provinces of Holland. Lord Sandwich had already returned to England with the fleet to refit for action. The cousins were now on the best of terms again: 'At dinner' (on the 5th) 'he did use me with the greatest solemnity in the world, in carving for me and nobody else and calling often to my Lady (Sandwich) to cut for me:

and all the respect possible.' This was a great weight off
Mr. Pepys' mind. He turned to face his work again in good
heart.

He found that Parliament had voted funds at last, to the
tune of two and a half million pounds, a vast sum in those days.
The war was expected to last three years. The Duke of York
was to go to sea in command of the naval forces, with Prince
Rupert and Lord Sandwich as his immediate subordinates.
Penn—who did not care for Sandwich—was to be Captain of
the Fleet under the Duke. The men-of-war and their auxiliaries
available for service on the Dutch coast would number a
hundred. The Duke of Albemarle, formerly General George
Monk, that 'quiet, heavy man' according to the Diarist, would
remain ashore in charge of the Navy Office.

On the 30th of the month, having been very 'merry' with
Mrs. Martin only three days before, he found her 'mighty
reserved and resolved to keep herself so till the return of her
husband . . .' the reason being, rather strangely, that 'she is
informed he hath another woman whom he uses and has long
done, as a wife'. Samuel adds that it is 'a pleasant thing to think
of her'. The passage is rather cryptic. It may simply mean that
Betty Martin, as we must now call her, was in such a rage with
the delinquent purser that she did not feel like casual adultery
until she had had it out with him, and that Pepys was amused
by her highly moral attitude, which he knew would not last
long. It is likely, perhaps, that Mrs. Martin had solemnly
sworn to be chaste as an example to the faithless one. In any
case, she deliberately flaunted Samuel in his face as soon as
she got the chance. But whatever Betty meant by her temporary
stand-offish behaviour, it did not interrupt Sam's pleasant
intimacies with her for more than a few days.

On 12th April there was a romp at Lady Batten's. Pepys had
long considered her husband, the Commissioner, a 'knave', and
he really seems to have been rather an objectionable fellow,
though jovial enough on occasion. As for his wife, common
gossip had it that she was a 'whore', i.e. in our language, a

bitch who would stop at nothing to get her own way in sexual or any other matters.

The Battens were, however, rich and hospitable. Their so-called friends included the Penns, Sir William (with whom the other Sir William—Batten—was at daggers drawn) and his recently married wife, 'a well-looked, fat, short, old Dutch-woman, but one that hath been heretofore pretty handsome and is now very discreet and I believe hath more wit than her husband'. For Sam now rated Penn as low as he did Batten. Both families were nevertheless on fairly intimate terms with the Diarist and his wife, the Battens actually living next door to them—a circumstance which caused endless disputes between the two wives, mostly about the communal 'house of office', otherwise the privy.

At any rate that evening 'going to my lady Batten's there found a great many women with her, in her chamber merry, my lady Pen and her daughter among others; where my lady Pen flung me down upon the bed and herself and others, one after another, upon me and very merry we were . . . merry as I could be . . .' This was characteristic Restoration gaiety, of a kind peculiarly English, and perhaps Dutch, since a 'Dutch-woman' started this example of it, that has lasted in certain circles down to our own day. In horsey country houses and at Chelsea parties very similar scenes can be witnessed at the present time, when they are still described, significantly enough, as 'horseplay'. No one, incidentally, seemed worried about Lady Penn's original nationality, despite the officially declared war against the Dutch.

Just before the great English victory of 3rd June 1665, off Lowestoft, Mr. Pepys, after attending the funeral of a prominent London goldsmith, 'took coach and to Westminster Hall, where I took the fairest flower and by coach to Tothill Fields for the ayre till it was dark. I 'light and with the fairest flower to eat a cake and there did do as much as was safe with my flower and that was enough on my part. Broke up and away without any notice and after delivering the rose where it should be' (Westminster Hall, no doubt!) 'I to the Temple and 'light and . . . so home to write letters but very few God knows, being by my pleasure made to forget everything that is. The coachman that carried us cannot know me again nor the people at the house where we were.'

The Secretary's obsession with this sort of horticulture was beginning to be dangerous. Nowadays, before picking up a girl at Westminster, he had to look round to see whether the Duke of Albemarle, or perhaps Sir Philip Warwick, was safely out of sight. He had received many compliments from great and serious men lately for his honest and able conduct of naval business, and had even met the King himself. It would not do at all to have it known that he had been seen plucking 'roses' from the Hall and driving them off to Tothill Fields like such rakes as Sedley or Buckhurst. The Diarist's worldly ambitions took precedence even of his passion for pretty women; as a commoner he was not supposed to cultivate both impartially, though as a matter of fact he was quite determined to do so and thought it could be done with prudence, a virtue of which he knew himself to be in full possession. The cipher alone proves that point. And the Diary, added to the cipher and what we know of Pepys from other sources, proves that he got away with it. For more than a hundred years after his death, no one ever dreamed that this admirable public servant ever cast a libidinous eye upon 'flowers'.

On 8th June 'I met with the great news at last newly come . . . from the Duke of Yorke that we have totally routed the Dutch . . .' Mr. Pepys was told that the enemy 'neglecting greatly the opportunity of the wind they had of us . . . lost the benefit of their fireships'. These were vessels which in those days were set on fire to drift before the wind among the opposing ships as an alternative to gunfire.

The first report was mainly accurate. The battle had lasted all day with varying fortunes till at last the Dutch flagship was blown up and its admiral, Opdam, killed. Admiral Cornelius van Tromp, son of the Dutch admiral defeated by Blake in Cromwell's time, covered the Dutch retreat so skilfully that the Duke of York was not able, or daring or dexterous enough, to turn the victory into a rout.

Lord Sandwich, on the other hand, was said to have distinguished himself, and this item naturally delighted the Diarist. Sir William Coventry—he had been knighted just before the fleet sailed—wrote that the *Prince*, the earl's flagship, had been attacked by four of Opdam's men-of-war at once, but had eventually been rescued by four of the Duke of York's own squadron. Sandwich had immediately signalled the ships behind him to make for the Dutch at full speed. His entire squadron had charged, their guns blazing and their fireships aflame, throwing the whole of the enemy line into confusion.

In a few minutes several of the Dutchmen had been grappled, boarded and captured, and by dusk the rest had been in full retreat towards Holland; but according to Coventry pursuit had been countermanded by some mistake while the Duke of York was asleep. This excuse sounds rather thin, the loyal defence of a respected chief by a man who had been so long and closely associated with him. No commander-in-chief has any business to be asleep in battle. The Dutch were said to have lost thirty of their ships, but the whole fleet might well have been annihilated if the Duke had been more vigilant, to say the least of it.

Samuel naturally expressed no opinion on the Duke's conduct. He was no seaman, though he knew a lot about naval life ashore. To him the great victory had been a personal triumph for his cousin, whose star would now inevitably be in the ascendant—with Sam, Sam hoped, accompanying him to glory. The Clerk of the Acts congratulated himself again and again that he and the earl had parted on such friendly terms. He rushed down to the Nore to board the battered *Prince* and kiss his Lord's hand as soon as the flagships made the estuary.

But the year 1665 was not by any means over yet. It was to be one of the most terrible the country had ever experienced, and to show Samuel in a new light, not that cast by blazing guns or bright eyes, but the pallid and lethal gleam of a horror no man could foresee or repel, one that struck high and low, at any moment of day or night, and generally killed where it struck.

5

Under the Plague

THAT month the first red crosses, signs of the Great Plague, appeared upon doors in Drury Lane, with the words 'Lord have mercy upon us', written below the ominous symbols. Rejoicings over the victory at sea turned peoples' minds in other directions for the time being. But the gaieties of London were to be struck cruel blows during the next few months, and in the general terror the Clerk of the Acts was to be left almost alone to manage naval affairs. He rose to the occasion; nothing in Sam Pepys is more admirable than the courage and industry he showed during this fearful period.

Visits to such taverns as the Swan and the Harp and Ball near Whitehall, with the usual kissing and fondling of the potmaids there, continued at odd moments. But they are now often reported with the significant phrase, *un peu de temps con la fille*, meaning that the busy Secretary could not stay long. It is therefore unlikely that Mr. Pepys' amours were proceeding at the same accelerated tempo as hitherto.

It was no wonder that he felt slowed down. Persons of a more reckless temper, both men and women, reacted to this devastating epidemic of bubonic plague by calling, like *fin de siècle* poets, for 'madder music and for stronger wine', to say nothing of more frequent copulation. Wild revels had been held before in Europe on these occasions, especially in Italy in Boccaccio's time and later. But although Samuel often records that he was 'merry' during the summer months of 1665 and the spring of 1666, his festivities were generally politic rather than heartfelt. His basically sober character, with its dislike of every species of disorder except that under the star of Venus, could only be depressed and horrified by what he saw and heard of this terrible scourge in London.

The early signs of infection were hard sores surrounded by a crimson ring, which might appear anywhere on the body. By 15th June the mortality statistics admitted to 112 deaths, the real figure being probably much higher. Two days later 'It struck me very deep this afternoon going with a hackney coach from my Lord Treasurer's down Holborne, the coachman I found to drive easily and easily, at last stood still, and come down hardly able to stand, and told me that he was suddenly struck very sicke, and almost blind, he could not see; so I 'light and went into another coach, with a sad heart for the poor man and trouble for myself, lest he should have been struck with the plague, being at the end of the towne that I took him up; but God have mercy upon us all!'

On the 21st 'I find all the towne almost going out of towne, the coaches and waggons being all full of people going into the country'. The doctors and magistrates were helpless. All they could do was to impose quarantine, order the slaughter of domestic animals, and fumigate premises where deaths had taken place. The whole of the parish of St. Giles, the worst infected district, was isolated, but the disease spread steadily towards the heart of the City and Mr. Pepys' own quarters. Samuel walked about chewing tobacco and travelled as much as he could by water.

Early in July he sent his wife to live at Woolwich, considered safer from the plague. The usual loneliness, with its inevitable result, ensued. Unfortunately most of the well-known London pleasure resorts were now closed, and many houses in 'gay' districts had shut their doors. Woolwich, however, was not 'in the country', and Mr. Pepys found time to run down there by water for an occasional night or two. Moreover, Mary, a maid at the Harp and Ball, whose surname the Diarist does not condescend to mention, at last 'with much ado' consented to go out with him. He left a solemn Trinity House banquet before it was half over to keep the appointment 'at the New Exchange, and there took coach and I with great pleasure took the ayre to Highgate and thence to Hampstead, much pleased with her company, pretty and innocent, and had what pleasure almost I would with her, and so at night, weary and sweaty, it being very hot beyond bearing, we back again and I set her down in St. Martin's Lane.'

This vivid passage seems positively to refer to an event of only yesterday, the one difference being that the young Civil Servant and the barmaid made their excursion to Hampstead Heath by horse transport instead of in the gentleman's sports car. There was also a girl named Nan, employed at a tavern in Mortlake and apparently the wife of a sailor, with whom Sam was 'very much pleased and merry' about this time. But 'above 700 died of the plague this week' (13th July 1665). This number had nearly doubled a few days later.

But public affairs had to go on. The fleet again sailed out to look for the Dutch, Sandwich in command. The Duke of York was to remain in England, at the King's orders, ostensibly because his life was too valuable to risk, but really on account of his poor showing at the battle of Lowestoft. Prince Rupert, whose own behaviour at the battle had not been much better, had declined to share responsibility at sea with a mere earl. Consequently, the fate of the country depended largely on the two cousins, Sandwich the fighting seaman and Samuel Pepys, the Director, as we might call him today, of naval supplies.

There were other noblemen and gentlemen who were less concerned with the fate of the country than with their own. The plague had reached Whitehall, and the courtiers were packing up to take refuge at their rural seats. By the end of the month the King himself had moved to Hampton, leaving the imperturbable Duke of Albemarle in charge of the capital. The London shops were mostly shuttered. Watchmen picketed the infected houses. The streets, formerly so crowded, were half empty by this time. There was plenty of room for the death-carts, preceded by constables with red staves, chanting their deep and hoarse cry of 'Bring out your dead!', while outside the City walls great pits had been dug in the fields for the ever-increasing loads of naked corpses.

Sam kept his head in one sense. He was not frightened of the 'pest'; he made his will and 'put all things in order', including periodical visits to and from Mrs. Bagwell. He also, on 6th August, a Sunday, took some liberties with the youngest of his maids, of whom he now had four. 'Dressed and had my head combed by my little girle, to whom I confess—' here follows a jumble of French, Spanish and Latin words, meaning that he couldn't help slipping his hands into her corsage— '*que je sum demasiado kind, nuper ponendo mes mains in su des choses de son* breast, *mais il faut que je* leave it, lest it bring me to *alcun* major inconvenience.' Mrs. Pepys, after all, was not so very far away. As already noted the servants in a middle-class London household of the seventeenth century were much more like members of the family than they afterwards became. One of the regular domestic rows might easily lead to highly 'inconvenient' revelations by a party who felt herself injured, not so much by the wandering hands of her master as by the reckless or possibly justified accusations, on quite a different subject, of her mistress.

Sam still could not keep away from half desolate Westminster Hall, but he only heard 'very sad stories' there, of many old friends who had died or left, and he made up his mind at last to cut out visits to that once gay quarter. By 10th August the weekly death-rate had risen to the appalling figure of over 3,000, 'the town growing so unhealthy that a man cannot depend upon living two days to an end'. But the worried Secretary never dreamed of deserting his post, as even the King had. Samuel could have easily pretended that he must have a holiday and go down to his father's house at Brampton 'for a few days', which he could as easily have extended to months. But there is not the slightest sign of panic, though many of sympathy and horror, in any of his entries in the Diary this year.

From another point of view, that of Sam's advancement in his career, it might seem risky for him to entertain Mrs. Bagwell in his office, as he did this month. But the times were so disturbed, what with the Dutch war and the plague, and there were so many visitors of all kinds to the Navy Office, including many women, that the Secretary did as he pleased in his private room. On the 11th 'a pleasant recontre happened in having a young married woman brought me by her father . . . to get her husband off that he should not go to sea, *une contre pouvait avoir* done any *cose cum elle* but I did nothing *si ni biasser* her'. This extraordinary language means that Pepys could have had intercourse with the lady there and then if he had chosen, but contented himself with a mere kiss. Prudence, as so often with this amorist, won the day for the moment. Yet 'after they were gone my mind run upon having them called back again and I sent a messenger to Blackwall, but he failed. So I lost my expectation.' But about a fortnight later he succeeded in it.

The reflections of this intrepid, optimistic and energetic man on the plague took a bizarre form on the 15th. 'Something put my last night's dream into my head, which I think is the best that ever was dreamt, which was that I had my lady Castlemayne in my armes and was admitted to use all the dalliance I desired with her, and then dreamt that this could not be awake, but that it was only a dream; but that since it was a dream and that I took so much real pleasure in it, what a happy thing it would be if when we are in our graves (as Shakespeere resembles it) we could dream and dream but such dreams as this, that then we should not need to be so fearful of death as we are this plague time.'

This deduction from Hamlet's famous speech is so character-istic of the Diarist that, if it were not so long, it could almost stand as a motto for the present narrative.

Meanwhile, however, Mrs. Bagwell proved a very acceptable substitute for Lady Castlemaine. Visits to Deptford, recorded, as was now usual with Sam, in a weird mixture of canine French, Spanish and Latin, were regular, and seem by this time to have been recognised by the whole family—including the lady's father and mother, if not yet her husband—as part of the natural order of things. It was therefore doubly agreeable to Samuel when, on the 19th, the King ordered the Navy Office to remove from the Tower district down river to the safer area of Greenwich, practically next door to Deptford, though a little further east.

It was not so agreeable, on the 21st, to find that the lodgings 'appointed for us there for our office . . . do by no means please me, they being in the heart of all the labourers and workmen there, which makes it as unsafe as to be, I think, at London'. Congested districts are of course more liable to be hard hit in times of epidemic. Mr. Pepys may also have been thinking of the possibility of riots in these disturbed times, when the chronic shortage of money, the long hours of work and the depletion of staffs by disease were already leading to serious discontent among the men who repaired the ships and loaded the stores.

After inspecting these premises he paid a visit to Elizabeth at Woolwich, three miles down the river. As he could not obtain transport, 'I was forced to walk it in the darke, at ten o'clock at night, with Sir J. Minnes's George' (a servant) 'with me, being mightily troubled for fear of the doggs at Coome farme and more for fear of rogues by the way, and yet more because of the plague which is there' (i.e. at the farm) 'which is very strange, it being a single house, all alone from the towne, but it seems they use to admit beggars, for their owne safety, to lie in their barns, and they brought it' (the plague) 'to them; but I bless God I got about eleven of the clock well to my wife . . .' He was never allowed to forget the horrors of the epidemic. On his way to Greenwich on the 22nd 'in my way seeing a coffin with a dead body therein, dead of the plague, lying in an open close belonging to Coome farme, which was carried out last night and the parish have not appointed any body to bury it; but only set a watch there day and night, that nobody should go thither or come thence, which is a most cruel thing; this disease making us more cruel to one another than if we are doggs'.

It is a sensitive and just comment. But a few hours later the man who had made it was hanging round the King's Yard, on the look-out for Mrs. Bagwell. 'Walked up and down and by and by out at the back gate and there saw the Bagwell's wife's mother and daughter and went to them and went into the daughter's house and *faciebam le cose que ego tenebam* a mind to *con elle*' (did the things I had a mind to with her) 'and drinking and talking, by and by away . . .'

That week over 6,000 persons died of the plague, officially, but Pepys fears the actual number is nearer 10,000, 'partly from the poor that cannot be taken notice of through the greatness of the number and partly from the Quakers and others that will not have any bell ring for them'. The numbers went on rising until the middle of September, when they began to fall.

But even on the 14th of that month he draws up a melancholy catalogue. 'My meeting dead corpses of the plague, carried to be buried close to me at noonday through the City in Fanchurch Street. To see a person sick of the sores carried close by me by Gracechurch in a hackney coach. My finding the Angel tavern at the lower end of Tower hill shut up and more than that, the alehouse at the Tower stairs and more than that the person was then dying of the plague when I was last there, a little while ago at night, to write a short letter there and I overheard the mistress of the house sadly saying to her husband somebody was very ill, but did not' (i.e. Sam did not) 'think it was of the plague. To hear that poor Payne, my waiter, hath buried a child and is dying himself. To hear that a labourer I sent but the other day to Dagenhams, to know how they did there, is dead of the plague and that one of my own watermen, that carried me daily, fell sick as soon as he had landed me on Friday morning last, when I had been all night upon the water . . . and is now dead of the plague . . .'

The Secretary's life was in more danger than if he had been with the fleet in the North Sea; but if he flinched a little occasionally, he still thought of others more than of himself. 'But, Lord!' he writes of the Moorfields district in London, where many corpses were buried, 'how every body's looks and discourse in the street is of death and nothing else and few people going up and down, that the towne is like a place distressed and forsaken.' On 31st August he notes: 'thus this month ends with great sadness upon the publick, through the greatness of the plague everywhere through the kingdom almost. Every day sadder and sadder news of its encrease.'

Nevertheless, on the 2nd September, 'After dinner I to Deptford and there took occasion to *entrar a la casa de la gunaica de ma Minusier* and did what I had a mind . . .' The foreign words meaning 'enter the house of my carpenter's wife' start in Spanish, continue in transliterated Greek and end in French. Pepys' classical education at St. Paul's and Magdalene helped him with his Spanish, which had been the second language of Englishmen—French, as usual, being the first— ever since their pirates had begun to plunder the Spanish Main in the previous century.

On 7th September deaths from the plague reached an official record of close on seven thousand, 'which is a most dreadfull number and shows reason to fear that the plague hath got that hold that it will yet continue among us'. For all he knew it was going to spread across the entire country, as the Black Death had done in the fourteenth century; in fact, it was to last several months longer, though gradually abating. Meanwhile Mr. Pepys went steadily on with his work.

He soon had even more to think about. On the 10th news came in that Lord Sandwich had distinguished himself again. In the best traditions of the Navy he had dashed in among the perilous shallows of the Dutch coast to surprise a fleet of East Indiamen, their officers never dreaming that he would take such a risk. He captured two of the great merchantmen and four men-of-war. Next day he repeated the feat, taking four more fighting ships and two more of the East Indiamen. A storm got up and prevented further operations. But in the end Sandwich sailed back to the Nore with no less than 13 prizes, all their cargoes intact.

There was a dispute about these cargoes later on. Sandwich, under pressure from Penn and others, allowed his officers to take a share of well over 5 per cent of the total value—half a million sterling—of spoil and meanwhile the ordinary seamen stripped the decks, as they were entitled to, amid scenes recalling a mutiny; some of them were even shot by the guards set to keep them off the officers' part of the plunder. Pepys himself got a share worth £500.

However, some of the more straight-laced flag officers reported Sandwich's breach of the regulations to the Council of State. Technically, he should not have allowed any of the prize cargo to be distributed except that on deck, the ordinary seamen's perquisite. The Duke of Albemarle ordered all goods on the prize ships to be impounded by the Customs. At this moment a strong Dutch fleet was reported off the English coast. Sandwich, on good naval grounds, refused to put to sea to meet it. He was right; a storm soon blew the Dutch away, and it was evident that their approach had been merely demonstrative. But Sandwich's enemies now had two counts against him. Words very like 'thief' and 'coward' were heard in private.

That autumn mortality from the plague decreased slightly. But its effect upon society, coupled with the anxieties of the war, remained disastrous. Refinement, as is usual in times of such disorders, almost ceased to exist, except in a few circles to which Sam was admitted, notably that of his fellow-diarist, Mr. John Evelyn. The King appeared to be almost wholly given over to sexual dissipation. In October Pepys was quite shocked to hear from a colleague who spent much time at Court that Charles spent most of his with his feminine favourites 'feeling and kissing them naked', with some further unsavoury details that seemed to prove that the case was hopeless and the occupant of the British throne was utterly unfit for any sort of serious business.

Sam took the news with a pinch of salt. He was naturally a loyal subject; he liked the King personally—as everyone did—and continued to serve him as before. The Secretary knew from his own experience that a very strong interest in good-looking young women could quite well be compatible with assiduous devotion to administrative work. His own virtues in this respect were signally rewarded on 27th October, on which date he dined with the grim Duke of Albemarle. 'He makes mighty much of me; and here he tells us the Dutch are gone . . . through the last foul weather. Here he proposed to me from Mr. Coventry' (this gentleman was already a knight, but Pepys could not get used to his new title) 'as I had desired of Mr. Coventry, that I should be Surveyor Generall of the Victualling business, which I accepted. But indeed the terms in which Mr. Coventry proposes it for me are the most obliging that ever I could expect from any man and more; it saying me to be the fittest man in England and that he is sure, if I will undertake, I will perform it; and that it will be also a very desirable thing that I might have this encouragement, my encouragement in the Navy alone being no wise proportionable to my pains or deserts. This, added to the letter I had three days since from Mr. Southerne' (Sir William Coventry's secretary) 'signifying that the Duke of Yorke had in his master's absence opened my letter' (to Coventry) 'and commanded him to tell me that he did approve of my being the Surveyor General, do make me joyful beyond myself that I cannot express it, to see that as I do take pains, so God blesses me and hath sent me masters that do observe that I take pains.'

This was the biggest testimonial that Mr. Pepys had received from the authorities so far. It was a well-deserved one. Even if the Duke of York, Sir William and the Duke of Albemarle had read the whole of the ciphered Diary to date, and thus been apprised in detail of the Secretary's little games, so frankly recorded, with the wives of their pursers, carpenters and other minor servants of the Navy, there is not the slightest doubt that the magnates in question would have remained enthusiastic about Sam's administrative qualifications—which would have brought him high in any age, perhaps, but those of the late nineteenth century or mid-twentieth.

He wished that it had been through Lord Sandwich that he had received the appointment, though he greatly respected Coventry. Unfortunately these two important men were enemies, and of the two it was now his cousin who was on the down-grade, after having been, so short a time before, a national hero. It was a terrible pity, Sam thought, hoping

devoutly that Sandwich would understand the position and not
conclude that his ambitious relative was cynically deserting him
for Sir William. All the same, it was going to be very difficult
to walk the tightrope between Coventry and the earl. Playing
off one girl against another would be nothing to it.

How these courtiers did quarrel, to be sure! Samuel really
deplored the deterioration in manners of the aristocracy in
particular, even when it happened to suit his own irrepressible
sensuality. On the evening of 13th November he and a friend
visited the house of a Mr. Glanvill, where they found a 'very
fine, witty lady', one Judith Penington, daughter of an alderman
and sister of an eminent Quaker. 'There he and I sat talking and
playing with Mrs. Penington, whom we found undrest in her
smocke and petticoats by the fireside, and there we drank and
laughed, and she willingly suffered me to put my hand in her
bosom very wantonly and keep it there long. Which methought
was very strange and I looked upon myself as a man mightily
deceived in a lady, for I could not have thought she could have
suffered it, by her former discourse with me; so modest she
seemed and I know not what.' Not one of Mr. Pepys' former
or current mistresses would have dreamed of permitting such
familiarity before a third person; moreover this was only the
third time he had ever even seen Mrs. Penington, who seems to
have been unmarried at the time. The reaction from the ferocious
puritanism of the Cromwellian interlude, the subsequent almost
hysterical welcome to a Frenchified Royal Court, followed by the
coincidence of an expensive war and a new Black Death, had
disagreeably coarsened English behaviour, so that both men
and women were not only more licentious but also more cruel
and callous than they had ever been before.

Even the young girls had become quite complaisant. 'Little
Mrs. Frances Tooker', who had a mother still able to attract
the insatiable Diarist, allowed him to sit 'dallying with her an
hour, doing what I would with my hands about her. And a
very pretty creature it is.' Miss Tooker is elsewhere referred to
as 'almost a woman', which would mean in those days that she
was not marriageable, i.e. under fifteen. She was also quite well

known to Mrs. Pepys, and on one occasion actually slept in the Diarist's house, though not, apparently, with himself. Female children of this age would never have been left alone with a man, let alone have come to him of their own free will, ten years before this date. Elizabeth Pepys did not seem to care, jealous though she was of adult young women; perhaps even she did not dream that her hot-blooded spouse, as he grew older, would investigate the nursery as well as the drawing-room. It happened that in this case the mother, fond of pleasure herself, was not very strict with little Miss Frances, for a couple of years later Mrs. Pepys told her husband, whether with or without malice aforethought, that the child, still only about sixteen, had been infected with gonorrhoea.

Samuel, meanwhile, had by no means done with Judith Penington. On Sunday evening, 26th November 'I stayed alone talking and playing with her till past midnight, she suffering me whatever *ego voulais avec ses mamilles* . . . much pleased with her company we parted . . .' The unprinted portion of the text at this point refers to a good deal more than breast-fondling. Judith was Sam's first really sophisticated mistress. She probably extended the range of his erotic practices considerably.

On 4th December 'late by water home, taking a barrel of oysters with me, and at Greenwich went and sat with Madam Penington . . . and made her undress her head and sit dishevilled all night sporting till two in the morning . . .' Where Mrs. Penington is concerned the MS. is generally too explicit for printing. At this period she quite eclipses the humble and modest Mrs. Bagwell, who is not heard of again in the Diary until the following June.

But Judith was not always so forthcoming. A few days before Christmas 1665 'I to Mrs. Penington and had a supper from the King's Head for her and there mighty merry and free as I used to be with her and at last, late, I did pray her to undress herself into her nightgowne, that I might see how to have her picture drawne carelessly' (i.e. in *négligée*) '(for she is mighty proud of that conceit) and I would walk without in the streete till she had done. So I did walk forth and whether I made too many turns or no in the darke cold frosty night between the two walls up to the Parke gate I know not, but she was gone to bed when I come again to the house upon pretence of leaving some papers there, which I did on purpose by her consent.'

The disappointment did not last long. No sooner had Samuel reached home that night when he found another pretty girl waiting to see him, on the business, however, of obtaining the Surveyor's interest in the promotion of her husband to the rank of Lieutenant in the Navy. This was Mrs. Daniel, a neighbour in whom Pepys had recently begun, in fact, to be interested, and whom he had invited to supper and cards, with some other ladies and little Frances Tooker, a day or two before. 'I had the opportunity here of kissing her again and again and did answer that I would be very willing to do him any kindnesse and so parted . . .' By this time Samuel was kissing practically all his lady clients—provided they were pretty, of course—of whom there were several with naval husbands or brothers to be promoted or prevented from going to sea by the Surveyor's influence.

The plague was now abating, as the weather grew colder. The shops began to re-open. Traffic, both commercial and private, increased, and the streets became more animated. By the new year of 1666 London life was waking up a little. But the King and the Court still came no nearer to the capital than Hampton. Samuel was glad to hear that Sandwich was on good terms with the monarch, if not with the Duke and the Coventry-Albemarle faction. Charles had tactfully arranged for the earl to go as a special ambassador to Spain with the object of holding Louis XIV in check at that Court.

On 2nd January there was a party at Lord Brouncker's, where Samuel met 'my dear Mrs. Knipp—' this interesting actress's name is spelt in six different ways in the playbills of the period. She had a 'brute of a husband', whom Pepys calls a 'horse jockey'—'with whom' (the wife, not the husband) 'I sang and in perfect pleasure I was to hear her sing . . .' while

Sir John Minnes, the Comptroller of the Navy—a jocular character variously described by the Diarist at different times as a 'fine gentleman and a good scholar', 'an old coxcomb', and 'a doating fool', while Sir William Coventry once compared him to a lapwing, for 'all he did was to keepe a flutter, to keepe others from the nest that they would find', i.e. wanted all the perquisites for himself—'was in the highest pitch of mirthe and his mimicall tricks that ever I saw and most excellent pleasant company he is and the best mimique that ever I saw and certainly would have made an excellent actor and now would be an excellent teacher of actors'.

The busy Secretary had to leave this gay scene for a while to attend to his letters, but 'longing for more of her company' (i.e. Mrs. Knipp's) 'I returned and met them coming home in coaches, so I got into the coach where Mrs. Knipp was and got her upon my knee (the coach being full) and played with her breasts and sung, and at last set her at her house and so good-night'. It is a pretty picture and would be very twentieth-century if we substituted cars for the coaches. By this time Sam was as much at home in this smart society of aristocrats and stars of the theatre as he had long been in equally boisterous if humbler circles. The latter soon beckoned him again now that the shutters were going up at the west end of the town, goods and sparkling eyes were on sale once more, or even to be had for nothing if one knew the ropes, while the gallants and their milliners returned to swarm in the taverns and along the river walks.

At Westminster Hall, in February, 'I hear that Mrs. Lane is come to town. So I staid loitering up and down till anon she comes and agreed to meet at Swayn's and there I went anon and she come but staid but little, the place not being private. I have not seen her since before the plague. So thence parted and *rencontrais* at her last *logis* and in the place did what I *tenais a* mind *pour ferais con* her. At last she desired to borrow money of me, £5, and would pawn gold with me for it, which I accepted and promised in a day or two to supply her.' In spite of these renewed relations with one of his most admired

mistresses, who seems to have had a very special attraction for
him—since he returned to her, after quarrels, again and again—
Samuel felt understandably uneasy at having entered two
houses, Swayn's tavern and Betty Lane's own old lodgings,
which had been shut up for months on account of deaths there
from the plague.

But a few days later 'met at her chamber and there did what
I would' as before, but not in Franco-Spanish this time.
The same evening he returned with the loan of £5 for which
she had asked, 'and then did what I would with her and I
perceive she is come to be very bad, and offers any thing, that
it is dangerous to have to do with her, nor will I see her any
more a good while'. Betty Lane's sojourn in the country did
not seem to have improved her morals; or at any rate, by now
she made less of a secret of their real nature to her remarkably
loyal lover. She must have known that however much her
behaviour might shock him, he could never do without her for
long. In fact, the 'good while' Sam promised himself on
1st March came to an abrupt end on the 18th.

That afternoon Betty's husband, Mr. Martin, was at home.
He seems to have been no better than a pimp, for as soon as
he recognised the visitor he went out to get some wine, and left
the lovers quite long enough for them to 'do as they would',
in Samuel's favourite phrase. 'The poor man I do think would
take pains if I can get him a purser's place, which I will
endeavour—' Martin was apparently out of a job again, like
the ne'er-do-well he was. They were really a most disreputable
couple by this time, and it is a wonder that the prudent and
ambitious Surveyor, who had shaken hands with the King and
was on excellent terms with the Duke of York and many
other great gentlemen, could bear to keep in with them. But
it is obvious enough that he found Mrs. Lane physically
irresistible.

'She tells me as a secret,' he goes on, 'that Betty Howlet of
the Hall' (another little milliner at Westminster) 'my little
sweetheart, that I used to call my second wife, is married to a
younger son of Mr. Michell's (his elder brother, who should

have had her, being dead of this plague) at which I am glad and that they are to live nearer me in Thames Streete, by the Old Swan.' Michell, whom Pepys knew well, was a Westminster dealer in a number of commodities. We have already seen that the fine gentlemen who came to Westminster Hall to flirt with the shopgirls and maids were always delighted when the latter married—into comparative freedom—and often themselves engineered such marriages, as Sam himself had more than once done. He was to see and touch a good deal of Betty Michell in the months to come.

6

Private and Public Mischief

THE spring of 1666 proved warm. The plague returned, and the new Surveyor of Victualling had to work in his office like a nigger. The whole government was at sixes and sevens after spending two million pounds in attempts to destroy the Dutch fleet—attempts which had been unsuccessful, in spite of two victories. Albemarle was determined to do better in future. In the absence of Sandwich, in Spain, he was going to lead the fleet himself, in joint command with Prince Rupert. He warned the Surveyor sternly that there must be no mistake over supplies. Pepys bent his head. But 'God forgive me,' he writes, 'I do still see that my nature is not to be quite conquered, but will esteem pleasure above all things. Music and women I cannot but give way to, whatever my business is.'

At last, after more than one failure, he succeeded in finding Mrs. Martin (or Lane) at home. The well-worn phrase once more makes its appearance in the Diary. He spent most of the day, a Sunday, with her, but he 'was not well pleased with her over free and loose company'. This expression seems, as before, to suggest a certain coarsening of Betty's erotic conduct. Nevertheless, her censorious lover could not make up his mind to be rid of her. A fortnight later the phrase, in French this time, is in use again.

In smarter circles than Betty Martin's the talk was all of the 'amours and mad doings' at Court. Dr. Pierce told the Diarist 'how for certain Mrs. Stewart do do everything with the King that a mistress should do; and that the King hath many bastard children that are known and owned, besides the Duke of Monmouth'. It is, however, still not certain that Frances Stuart ever did yield to the King at this period, though she may well have done so after becoming Duchess of Richmond in the following spring.

Mrs. Pierce, for her part, contributed the story already referred to of her high and mighty friend, Mrs. Clerke, wife of the FRS, picking up a man in Westminster Hall and accompanying him to a brothel, where they stayed an unconscionable time.

As for the lower levels of society, Mr. Pepys 'spying out of my coach Jane that lived heretofore at . . . my barber's' (this was Jane Welsh, from whom Samuel had parted on unsatisfactory terms about a year before) 'I went a little further and stopped and went on foot back and overtook her, taking water at Westminster Bridge' (i.e. hiring a boat) 'and spoke to her and she telling me whither she was going I over the water and met her at Lambeth and there drank with her'. Jane told him that the man she had fallen in love with turned out to be married. However, she played the wronged and innocent heroine to little purpose with Samuel, for he left her, he says in Spanish and French, without 'trying to do anything'. It is not clear why his earlier intense passion for this Jane had cooled so decisively. Perhaps her looks and manners had degenerated with her fortunes, or the Diarist may have thought she had become too tough a character to associate with safely. At any rate, he never saw her again.

The fleet sailed on 23rd April. Samuel was pretty sure it was well equipped; if it did not do its work, that would be the fault of Albemarle and Rupert, neither of whom were seamen of the calibre of Lord Sandwich. He knew, of course, that if the Dutch got away again, or worse still won a battle, the Surveyor would be blamed. He collected his assets and made ready to depart in haste if necessary.

But at Deptford on 16th May, 'Lord!' he writes, 'to see with what itching desire I did endeavour to see Bagwell's wife, but failed, for which I am glad, only I observe the folly of my mind that cannot refrain from pleasure at a season above all others in my life requisite for me to shew my utmost care in.'

Four days later Betty Martin, though as submissive as ever, comes in for a further instalment of moral censure. 'I out to Westminster and straight to Mrs. Martin's and there did what I would with her, she staying at home all the day for me; and not being well pleased with her over free and loose company, I away . . .'

The case of Sam and this particular Betty is really rather remarkable. He not only despised her mentality, a natural enough reaction in so thoughtful a gentleman as Samuel, but also complains, apparently, of her too lascivious behaviour with himself. This reaction is certainly less natural, an unusual grievance in so keen an amorist. Yet of all his loves Betty Martin is the most constantly visited and entertained. In her case familiarity did not have to breed contempt, which was there almost from the start of their intimate relations. On the contrary, familiarity sharpened his appetite, if not his respect, for this mistress. There was something about her which we shall never know, which this otherwise frankest of diarists does not tell us even in cipher. All we can guess is that it was pretty certainly something purely physical.

England was now at war with France too. Towards the end of May there were rumours of a French fleet in the Channel, and Rupert sailed west to meet it with a third of the British ships. Admiral de Ruyter chose this moment to attack Albemarle in the Downs and a great battle began on 1st June, off the Gunfleet Sands. The guns could be heard clearly in London.

During the next two days Albemarle was gradually forced back, the Dutch having the advantage in numbers. On 4th June Rupert returned to reinforce the Duke, having found that the report of a French armada was false, but in the ensuing battle the English ships were eventually driven back into the Thames estuary with heavy loss. Invasion seemed imminent.

Even in those hectic days, while the Surveyor was facing charges by Prince Rupert of delay in supplies at Dover, the famous phrase of the Diary—'did what I would'—does service again, in English this time, and in rather an unexpected connection. On 7th June Mr. Pepys writes: 'home to dinner all alone . . . people being all gone to Woolwich . . . I left alone with little Mrs. Tooker, whom I kept with me in my chamber all the afternoon and did what I would with her.' The Diarist is not very explicit here. From what is said of the girl elsewhere it seems that (1) she was under the age of consent, (2) she was a social equal, a friend of the family who was constantly in the house, and (3) she was precocious, sitting down to cards with the adults and going with them to the theatre and so on. It is quite possible, therefore, that the Surveyor-General, now thirty-three years old, calmly seduced this child in his own home and that she was a virgin. But it is also conceivable that in so licentious a society she was nothing of the kind, especially as her mother's reputation was not un-sullied and the girl herself, next year, fell a victim to venereal disease. On occasions such as the meetings with Mrs. Lane, when there is no doubt that actual intercourse took place, the ominous phrase is usually, though not always, accompanied by a word in some language or other meaning 'all' or 'everything'. No such word is used in this case, and Pepys was quite capable, as other entries in the journal prove, of spending hours on end alone with a young woman simply 'playing'.

The only certain thing about this particular entry is that Sam did not think it a very important one. He immediately goes on to discuss at length the recent defeat at sea, of which he heard details from a male visitor that same afternoon. Moreover, subsequent references to Miss Tooker are casual in the extreme. On the whole it seems safe to conclude that Frances, even at the age of fourteen or fifteen, was already following in her mother's footsteps, and Sam merely did what most other men of his day and temperament would have done in the circumstances.

In some respects he was old-fashioned. He did not like some aspects of the new boldness and emancipation of women. On 12th June, 'Walking here' (in Whitehall) 'in the galleries I find the Ladies of Honour dressed in their riding garbs, with coats and doublets with deep skirts, just for all the world like mine, and buttoned their doublets up the breast, with perriwigs and with hats; so that, only for a long petticoat dragging under their men's coats, nobody could take them for women in any point whatever; which was an odde sight and a sight did not please me.'

Feeling the need of a complete change, he took a wherry to Deptford, but could not find the respectable Mrs. Bagwell, who did not go in for these grotesque fashions. Next day he had another try. 'The officers being gone in, returned and walked to Mrs. Bagwell's house and there (it being by this time pretty dark and past ten o'clock) went into her house and did what I would. But I was not a little fearfull of what she told me but now, which is, that her servant was dead of the plague, that her coming to me yesterday' (when they were both looking for each other, apparently, but in opposite directions) 'was the first day of her coming forth and that she had new whitened the house all below stairs, but that above stairs they are not so fit for me to go up to, they being not so. So I parted thence with a very good will, but very civil . . .'

The 'whitening' was by way of disinfectant. The prudent Diarist means here that he was glad to get away in these dangerous circumstances, but with his usual caution and self-command on such occasions he did not show his uneasiness. In point of fact, compared with some of his contemporaries, he behaved with exemplary fortitude and devotion to the public service during these disastrous years of epidemic at home and humiliation abroad.

In the same month he began to pay marked attention to Mary Mercer, his wife's maid, a superior sort of woman who had been in his service ever since September 1664. She played well on both harpsichord and viol, and also danced excellently. On the 19th, 'with my wife into the garden and there sang with Mercer, whom I feel myself begin to love too much by handling of her breasts in a' morning when she dresses me, they being the finest that ever I saw in my life, that is the truth of it.'

It appears that by this time Mrs. Pepys' jealousy had relaxed a good deal. The 'dressing' had probably more to do with Samuel's new 'perriwig', of which he was inordinately proud, than with any more intimate adjustments; the elaborate male costume of the period, however, always needed the touch of a feminine rather than a masculine valet. It was quite usual for husbands to be 'dressed' in this way by their wives' maids, on suitable occasions with accompanying 'dalliance' which no one concerned took at all seriously.

Although, shortly afterwards, Mary Mercer and Mrs. Pepys had a quarrel and the girl went home to her mother, the dispute does not seem to have concerned Sam, and was soon settled. The maid returned next day, much to the Diarist's relief.

On 12th July he indulged in a comparatively innocent excursion with a friend of Betty Martin's, a certain Mrs. Burroughs, the pretty widow of a naval officer, one of those who visited him in his office on business and were kissed almost as a matter of routine. 'I sent her away by agreement and presently I by coach after and took her up in Fenchurch Streete and away through the City, hiding my face as much as I could, but she being mighty pretty and well enough clad, I was not afeard, but only lest somebody should see me and think me idle. I quite through with her and so into the fields Uxbridge way, a mile or two beyond Tyburne, and then back and then to Paddington and then back to Lyssen green, a place the coachman led me to (I never knew in my life) and there we eat and drank and so back to Charing Crosse and there I set her down. All the way most excellent pretty company. I had her lips as much as I would and a mighty pretty woman she is and very modest and yet kind in all fair ways. All this time I passed with mighty pleasure, it being what I have for a long time wished for, and did pay this day 5s. forfeite for her company.'

The five shillings forfeit does not of course refer to payment for favours received, or even the expenses of the outing. The sum indicates the amount of a fine which Samuel privately imposed upon himself—a regular habit of his and a highly characteristic one—for neglecting his work on this occasion. From time to time he made 'vows', carefully noted, not to go 'abroad' with women, not to drink wine or not to go to the theatre, for certain periods. When he failed to keep these good resolutions, as he invariably did, he would solemnly deposit the amount of the 'forfeit' in a money-box.

Betty Martin had now moved to new lodgings, where Pepys visited her on the 25th 'and was with her close, but, Lord! how big' (i.e. pregnant) 'she is already. She is, or at least seems, in mighty trouble for her husband at sea, when I am sure she cares not for him, and I would not undeceive her, though I know his ship is one of those that is not gone' (with the rest of the fleet which had recently sailed to fight the Dutch) 'but left behind without men.' Mrs. Martin's hypocritical laments did not impress her lover any more than the rest of her conversation, which always bored him nowadays. It is only possible to guess at the real reason which kept him for ever hankering after her person.

On this very day, 25th July, the refitted English fleet forced de Ruyter's blockade of the Thames, and brought his squadrons to action off the North Foreland in Kent. The Dutch were routed with as heavy a loss as they had inflicted on the English a few weeks earlier. Albemarle pursued the enemy to the coast of Holland and destroyed a large number of merchantmen in the Vlie channel, as well as many storehouses ashore.

Before full details of this substantial victory reached London the man partly responsible for it was already on the warpath in another direction. On 1st August 'I to Mrs. Martin's, but she abroad, so I sauntered to or again to the Abbey and then to the parish church, fearfull of being seen to do so' (in case someone should report him to the office for idling) 'and after dinner to Mrs. Martin's and there find Mrs. Burroughs and by and by comes a pretty widow, one Mrs. Eastwood, and one Mrs. Fenton, a maid; and here merry kissing and looking on their breasts and all the innocent pleasure in the world. But, Lord! to see the dissembling of this widow, how upon the singing of a certain jigg by Doll, Mrs. Martin's sister, she seemed to be sick and fainted and God knows what because the jigg which her husband (who died this last sickness) loved. But by and by I made her as merry as is possible and towzled and tumbled her as I pleased and then carried her and her sober pretty kins-woman Mrs. Fenton home to their lodgings . . . and there left them. Mightily pleased with this afternoon's mirth but in great pain to ride in a coach with them for fear of being seen.'

This revel, with the Surveyor in full cry after five young women at once, rather cruelly ignoring the possibly genuine distress of one of them and soon drying her tears with his boisterous attentions, is highly characteristic of the manners of the age. The girls, except Mrs. Burroughs were all from shops or domestic service, not exactly prostitutes, but out for all they could get out of fine gentlemen. The visitor, for his part, was not exactly brutal, but thoroughly callous about what the ladies might be feeling, and intent only on 'mirth'.

Early that August Mrs. Pepys again began to cause Sam concern with her jealous fits. While his two great friends, Mary Knipp the actress and the ultra-smart Mrs. Pierce, were ostensibly being entertained at the Navy Office house by husband and wife together, Elizabeth suddenly started sulking. 'By and by she fell into some silly discourse wherein I checked her, which made her mighty pettish and discoursed mighty offensively to Mrs. Pierce, which did displease me.'

He controlled his anger, and tried to pass his wife's rudeness off as a joke. Elizabeth had hinted very strongly that she knew her guest had criticised her clothes, suggesting that she was overdressed. Mrs. Pierce retorted smoothly that Mrs. Pepys should not worry about such foolish gossip, for Mrs. Pierce herself often had to put up with it, hearing, for example, only the other day that some absurd female had said she was lame. The remark, as everyone in the room knew, had been made by Elizabeth 'twenty times'.

The atmosphere, consequently, grew somewhat heavy. Mary Knipp good-humouredly suggested some music. She and Samuel sang. Then the guests said they must go, and the host proposed that he and Elizabeth should see them both home.

Elizabeth, with her chin in the air, refused to come, 'which vexed me'. Sam sent for a coach and took the other two women to a restaurant. He again apologised for his wife's conduct, which his guests admitted they considered rather odd, though they were polite enough and malicious enough to add that persons much inferior to Mrs. Pepys—for instance Mrs. Williams, Lord Brouncker's whore of a mistress—often went on like that. The notorious character in question, they said, had even once gone so far as to faint on the spot with rage.

Samuel reports all this rather innocently, being 'mightily pleased with the discretion of (Mrs. Pierce) during the simplicity and offensiveness of my wife's discourse this afternoon'. When he got home Elizabeth started all over again, 'reproaching of Mrs. Pierce and Knipp as wenches and I know not what. But I did give her no words to offend her and quietly let all pass and so to bed without any good looke or words to or from my wife.' Mrs. Pepys was really sometimes quite insufferable—enough to drive a far less susceptible student of young women than her husband 'abroad'.

The plague and the Dutch war had hit London hard enough, but now a third calamity fell upon the citizens which looked like outdoing both the others. On Sunday, 2nd September, 'some of our mayds sitting up late last night to get things ready against our feast to-day' (but that little party proved less pleasurable than expected) 'Jane called us up about three in the morning to tell us of a great fire they saw in the City. So I rose and slipped on my night-gowne and went to her window and thought it to be on the back-side of Marke Lane at the farthest . . .'

He did not consider they were in any danger, and went back to bed. But next day news came that three hundred houses had been burned down in the night, and that the fire was still raging near London Bridge. Mr. Pepys went 'abroad' to see for himself. He realised at once that the flames were spreading, and that there was panic in the City, 'Everyone endeavouring to remove their goods and flinging into the river or bringing them into lighters that lay off; poor people staying in their houses as long as till the very fire touched them and then running into boats or clambering from one pair of stairs by the water-side to another . . .'

Nobody seemed to be bothering to take any counter-measures. Pepys rushed to Whitehall, managed to see the King and the Duke of York and told them the only chance was to pull down the houses to windward of the path of the flames. He was asked to carry orders to the Lord Mayor accordingly. 'At last met my Lord Mayor in Canning Street, like a man spent, with a handkercher about his neck. To the King's message he cried, like a fainting woman, "Lord! What can I do? I am spent: people will not obey me. I have been pulling down houses; but the fire overtakes us faster than we can do it." ' The Mayor said he had been up all night and went off to have a rest, scandalising the conscientious Surveyor. Pepys heard later that the night before, when the alarm had first been given, the Lord Mayor had testily sent those who had awakened him about their business. 'Pish!' he was said to have grunted. 'This is no fire to wake a man for. A woman might piss it out.'

Sam himself returned home, 'in great trouble and disturbance', to meet his guests. The noonday meal to which he had invited them was well cooked and 'we were as merry as at this time we could be'. But all that day the wind and the flames roared; the streets were full of desperate citizens and the property they were trying to save, and the river was packed with barges and boats loaded to the water's edge. As the light waned the fire seemed more conspicuous and fiercer, 'in a most horrid malicious bloody flame, not like the fine flame of an ordinary fire'. Mr. Pepys wept at so much ruin in his beloved City.

'We were forced to begin to pack up our own goods and prepare for their removal.' No one slept that night. In the morning the Surveyor, still in his nightgown, took his money and plate in a cart lent him by Lady Batten to a friend's house in Bethnal Green, where the Penns and Battens had already deposited much of their own. On the 4th the confusion was temporarily increased by the thunder of explosions, as houses were blown up to save them from catching fire and thus increasing the area of catastrophe. Once they were down it was fairly easy to put out such flames as reached them, but that day the Old Bailey, Fleet Street, St. Paul's Cathedral and all Cheapside were reduced to blackened ruins.

Mr. Pepys slept on the floor in his office, 'being mighty weary and sore in my feet with going till I was hardly able to stand. About two in the morning my wife calls me up and tells me of new cryes of fire, it being come to Barkeing Church, which is the bottom of our lane.' On this intelligence they all left in a hurry for Woolwich, taking the Surveyor's savings, £2,350 in gold, with them in a friend's boat. The fire was at last beginning to come under some control, yet from the top of a church tower to which Samuel ascended he could see nothing but a desolate wilderness of destruction, 'all in dust'. The excitement, anxiety and sheer physical exhaustion had actually made so conscientious a Diarist forget the day of the week.

But, for all that, on the 6th he started to take a hand with the extinguishers. 'It was pretty,' he observes characteristically, 'to see how hard the women did work in the cannells' (the gutters) 'sweeping of water; but then they would scold for drink and be as drunk as devils. I saw good butts of sugar broke open in the street and people go and take handsfull out and put into beer and drink it.' That night he felt better, though still depressed by the general chaos, and managed to be 'mighty merry' at supper. He had done his duty, acted as King's messenger, saved his goods and the Navy Office, brought up labourers from the yards at Deptford and Woolwich and worked beside them with his own hands in the fire-fighting, while others panicked, transport and communications had come to a standstill and the Lord Mayor himself had gone to bed. Sam had a right to his relief and 'mirth'.

There had been no time to think of girls, but now the coast was clear again. On the 10th he looked up Mrs. Bagwell, but for some reason which he does not record she would not open the door to him. He returned the next day and made an appointment with her for the day after.

On the 12th, Mr. Pepys began to make up for lost time with a vengeance. He started with Betty Howlet, now Mrs. Michell, to whom he had been laying unsuccessful siege for many months. She told him, to his delight, that her husband had begun to be 'unkind' to her. 'I have promised to appear a counsellor to him. I am glad she is like to be so near us again.' In other words the usual technique for seducing young wives could now be set in motion in this case, especially as the Michells were in future to live nearer the Navy Office, their house having been burnt down in the late fire.

Next came the inevitable visit to Mrs. Martin. 'There did *tout ce que je voudrais avec* her . . . and then I found occasion to return in the dark and to Bagwell and there . . . (unprintable passage) . . . did do all that I desired, but though I did intend *pour avoir demeurais con elle* to-day last night, yet when I had done *ce que je voudrais* I did hate both *elle* and *la cose* and taking occasion from the occasion of *su marido's* return . . . (unprintable passage) . . . did *me lever* and so away home.' It certainly had been a strenuous day, especially after all the physical exhaustion of the previous week in dealing with the fire.

On 1st October, at Whitehall, 'did hear that Betty Michell was at this end of the towne and so without breach of vowe did stay to endeavour to meet with her and carry her home; but she did not come, so I lost my whole afternoon. But, pretty! how I took another pretty woman for her, taking her a clap on the breech, thinking verily it had been her.' It would have been amusing to have seen Samuel apologising for this mishap, which incidentally proves that he was already on fairly intimate terms with pretty Betty.

There were further visits this month to Mrs. Martin, in spite of her advanced pregnancy. On the 21st 'this afternoon I went to see and sat a good while with Mrs. Martin and there was her sister Doll, with whom, contrary to all expectation, I did what I would, and might have done anything else'. Here the famous phrase for once does not mean 'everything'. Presumably the presence of the sister longer established in Mr. Pepys' affections prevented a consummation. It is rather

remarkable that Betty Martin did not object to these pre-
liminaries; but she was a cynical young woman at heart, and,
after all, she was not in a fit condition to interfere seriously.
It is, perhaps, less remarkable that even at the bedside of an
expectant mother and current mistress the Surveyor should
have been unable to restrain his experimental fumblings. The
probability is that not one of the three of them considered the
demonstration at all improper.

A day or two later 'I down by water to Shadwell, to see
Betty Michell, the first time I was ever at their new dwelling
since the fire, and there find her in the house all alone. I find
her mighty modest. But had her lips as much as I would and
indeed she is mighty pretty and I love her exceedingly. I paid
her £10.1.0 that I received upon a ticket for her husband'
(i.e. a certificate that the Government owed him money as a
discharged seaman) 'which is a great kindness I have done
them, and having kissed her as much as I would I away, poor
wretch, and down to Deptford . . . Bagwell's wife, seeing me
come the fields way, did get over her pales to come and talk
with me, which she did for a good way and so parted . . .'

Progress was rather slow with Betty Michell, an unusually
circumspect young woman. Moreover, the reference to Mrs.
Bagwell sounds a little as though Mr. Pepys were getting tired
of her eternal petitions on behalf of her husband. Events were
following their normal course in such affairs. The seducer's
trump card was always his promise to improve the husband's
economic position. Sometimes he did and sometimes he didn't.
But if the lady gambled her virtue on the prospect, she often
assumed the right to refresh her lover's memory in and out of
season, which might or might not cause him to regret the whole
connection. On the whole the Surveyor did more to keep his
word than most gentlemen; but he was often distracted by the
complexities of his office, and never more so than at this time,
when, owing to the ignominious defeats at sea, a Parliamentary
enquiry into the conduct of the war was imminent.

He proceeded to make further trial of Doll Lane, Mrs.
Martin's sister. Only five days after the first test 'out, the first

time I ever was abroad with Doll Lane, to the Dog tavern, and there drank with her, a bad face, but good bodied girle. Did nothing but salute' (i.e. kiss) 'and play with her and talk . . .' For the moment he could not make up his mind about Doll, as she was not very 'pretty', but before long she joined his collection.

Meanwhile, Mrs. Bagwell's calls at the office, of which the Surveyor took the fullest possible advantage—'did what I would with her'—were renewed. Doll was taken to another tavern for talk and 'play', and her sister received a rare present, six bottles of claret, from the Diarist, possibly to console her for his attentions to Doll. Actually, Betty Martin does not seem to have been at all jealous. Their liaison was of such long standing that in any case such youthful recriminations would have been most inappropriate. On 24th November Mr. Martin told Pepys that Betty had been delivered of a female child, and the Diarist promised to 'christen' it the following Sunday.

But before then Mr. Pepys attempted and was accorded some familiarity by a girl of a rank actually superior to his own. Margaret, whom everyone called Peg, was the daughter of no less a magnate than Sir William Penn, Samuel's old friend and enemy. She was no beauty; in fact she was rather exceptionally plain, as the Diarist had briefly noted five years earlier, when he had first met her, fresh from school. But somehow or other—'home and there comes my lady Pen, Pegg and Mrs. Turner and played at cards and supped with us and were pretty merry, and Pegg with me in my closet a good while and did suffer me *a la baiser mouche*'. He does not mean what he says—that he gave her a 'fly' kiss, whatever that might be!—but simply that he kissed her on the *bouche*, 'mouth'. Pepys had learnt his French by ear. But also, he adds, in Franco-Spanish, '*et toucher ses cosas* upon her breast, wherein I had great pleasure'. The *cosas*, 'things', were the nipples, easily accessible below the 'handkercher' worn over the low-cut gowns of the period. Only a few days before the Diarist had sternly censured his wife for wearing this 'handkercher' too far down for what he considered decency.

Two days later he was at Westminster Hall again. 'I did go drink at the Swan and there did meet with Sarah' (waitress at the tavern) 'who is now newly married and there I did lay the beginnings of a future *amour con elle*' by taking some unprintable liberties with her. He had known and kissed Sarah for a year or two, but in accordance with his usual practice he had waited till she had got married before taking her seriously. The same evening 'called at Mrs. Burroughs' mother's door and she come out to me and I did *hazer* whatever I would . . .' Mrs. Burroughs was the widow he had taken on the excursion to Uxbridge and on similar outings since, without having hitherto made her his mistress. It is not to be supposed that he did more than 'towzle' her on this occasion, on a cold November night at her mother's door. The mis-spelt Spanish word used means simply 'do' (*hacer*).

He met Mrs. Burroughs again, with a very large company of Westminster friends, at the christening of Betty Martin's baby, to which he stood godfather. Betty Michell was also there. Sam, as a visiting celebrity, offered to drive some of the girls home, '. . . and no sooner in the coach but something broke, that we were fain there to stay till a smith could be fetched, which was above an hour, and then it costing me 6s. to mend. Away round by the wall and Cow Lane' (in Smithfield, then famous for coachmakers) 'for fear it should break again and in pain about the coach all the way. But to ease myself therein Betty Michell did sit at the same end with me . . .' (unprintable passage).

Next day 'away myself to Westminster Hall by appointment and there found out Burroughs and I took her by coach as far as the Lord Treasurer's and called at the cake house by Hales's and there in the coach eat and drank and then carried her home . . .' (more unprintable expressions) 'so having set her down in the place I to the Swan and there did the first time *baiser* the little sister of Sarah that is come into her place and so away by coach home . . . being weary of the following of my pleasure . . .'

In comparative affluence now, the Diarist was finding his obsession with Westminster and its gay feminine population rather more than he could manage with comfort. For he was still determined, 'pleasure' or no 'pleasure', to maintain his upward social progress. The double game naturally involved its fluctuations. But Samuel would not have been Samuel if he did not, as we shall see, keep it up—at any rate as long as he kept up his famous journal. After all, he had the conspicuous cautionary tale forever before his eyes of the sad conduct of King Charles II, 'the fittest man in the world to see all things well executed'—as he had shown at the time of the Great Fire— 'and yet hath no other employment but his lips about the Court', i.e. kissing its ladies.

7

Lengthening List

ALBEMARLE'S victory over the Dutch in the summer of 1666 had led to the initiation of peace feelers, which dragged on through the winter; both fleets were ostensibly laid up for repairs, though in reality the combatants were keeping a close watch on each other. But the English at least were hardly in a position to renew hostilities. In addition to their purely naval losses, which had been serious enough, the plague and the fire had disorganised administration. The admirals, the Court, the Navy Board and Parliament were in any case at mutual loggerheads. Accusations of corruption and incompetence, some of them well enough founded, were flying about like tennis balls; money was scarce, and tempers on edge. The seamen, who had not been paid for months, were on the verge of mutiny.

Samuel proved his innocence in all this quarrelling. He stuck to his proofs too. But Sir William Coventry resigned his commissionership on the Navy Board in disgust. So did Sir George Carteret, the Treasurer. These were about the only two men on the Board whom the Surveyor really liked and trusted. He was disturbed by these changes, but determined still to hold his own. While waiting for the Spring campaign—which in these circumstances could only be defensive, not calling for much in the way of supplies—Sam began to haunt Westminster Hall again.

He still remained on the best of terms with the Lanes, both Doll and Betty. The former seems to have become his mistress at the Bell tavern on 14th December. On the 18th 'to Westminster Hall to see Mrs. Martin, who is very well and intends to go abroad' (i.e. simply out of doors, the usual meaning of this word in the Diary) 'tomorrow after her childbed. She do tell me that this child did come *la meme jour* that it ought to *hazer* after my *avoir ete con elle* before her *marid* did *venir* home.' This polyglot cryptogram may be translated: 'Betty told me that her child had been conceived by my agency while her husband was away from home.' The Diarist makes no further comment, but coolly proceeds at once, 'Thence to the Swan and there I sent for Sarah and mighty merry we were . . .' to the extent that the rest of this passage is too obscene for print.

These gaps now begin to be rather frequent in the journal, relating both to girl callers on official business, Betty Michell in a coach, with her husband present but apparently unaware of what was going on, and Doll Lane. With the latter, at the Rose in Westminster, on 2nd January 1667 'we did *biber* a good deal *de vino et je* did give *elle* twelve *soldis para comprare elle* some gans for a new *anno's* gift . . .' i.e. they drank a lot and he gave her 12s. as a New Year's present. A veil must be drawn over their further proceedings on this occasion.

According to the Diary, the only girl whom both Pepys and his wife kissed at the same time was 'pretty, witty' Nell Gwyn. On 23rd January they saw her act, and very well, the part of Coelia in a 'silly play', *The Humerous Lieutenant*. After the performance Mr. and Mrs. Pepys were taken behind the scenes by friends and introduced to Nell, whom they promptly kissed, the gentleman, out of his vast experience in these matters, no doubt setting the example. He records that the kiss he gave Mrs. Gwyn 'specially' pleased him. At this time she was not yet Charles's mistress, but it may be assumed that she already knew a good deal about kissing.

The next evening Samuel threw a big dancing party at his house. The guests included the actress, Mrs. Knipp, who had introduced him to Nell Gwyn and whom of course he already knew quite well and admired greatly. 'Only towards morning Knipp fell a little ill and so my wife home with her to put her to bed and we continued dancing and singing . . .' Mary Mercer in particular being the life and soul of the party and 'made me in love with her more than ever'. 'The company being all gone to their homes I up with Mrs. Pierce to Knipp, who was in bed; and we waked her and there I handled her breasts and did *baiser la* and sing a song, lying by her on the bed . . . and so to bed myself, my mind mightily satisfied with all this evening's work and thinking it to be one of the merriest enjoyment I must look for in the world and did content myself therefore with the thoughts of it . . . only the musique did not please me, they not being contented with less than 30s.'

This highly characteristic entry, with its mixture of innocent and not so innocent 'merriment', musical criticism—they had Irish and Italian songs 'that did almost ravish me'—and final balancing of profit and loss, indicates in a nutshell the peculiar charm of Sam's personality, the primness of the solid citizen forming a perfect foil to the candidly, if confidentially, admitted lasciviousness. The pepper of the Diary's shocks is so inextricably mingled with the solid roast beef of common sense and the sweet sauce of a naïve romanticism that it seldom or never turns the severest reader's stomach. Much less obviously indecent writers, such as the next century produced—Laurence Sterne, for example—often leave a far more unpleasant taste in the literary mouth.

With Betty Michell, whom he did not often see alone, Mr. Pepys particularly enjoyed clandestine contacts. On the 27th January 'it being now dark and past six at night, I walked to the Swan in the Palace yard and there with much ado did get a waterman and so I sent for the Michells and they come and their father Howlett and his wife with them and there we drank and so into the boat, poor Betty's head aching. We home by water, a fine moonshine and warm night, it having been also a very summer's day for warmth. I did get her hand to me under my cloak . . .' (inevitable omission) 'so there we parted at their house and he walked almost home with me . . .' The entire family was by this time quite bewitched by the astute Diarist, who had delighted these relatively humble people by invitations to his own home and elsewhere, regularly treating them as social equals. On the 30th he brought his wife,

Mary Mercer and another maid to see them, the visitors taking their own provisions. But it was Mary he kissed that night, before going to bed, not Betty.

A call on Mrs. Bagwell—by the Surveyor alone, naturally—followed a couple of days later. Print, even in French and Spanish, must forgo the details. But a curious feature of this interview, indicating the open contempt for the husband shown so often by both parties in these affairs, is that when Mr. Bagwell turned up 'there without any notice taken by him we discoursed of our business of getting him the new ship building by Mr. Deane' (a Captain in the Navy, expert in naval construction) 'which I shall do for him'. The modest carpenter pretended not to be interested. Neither did the adulterous pair take the trouble to inform him what they were whispering about in his presence. It can hardly be doubted that Mr. Bagwell understood the true situation and cared little about his wife's infidelity, which after all paradoxically proved her love for him, so long as he obtained professional promotion. It is an old story, of course, repeated generation after generation, though not often in so blatant a form as here.

The same day 'it being now night, to Westminster Hall . . . and find Doll Lane and *con elle* I went to the Bell Taverne, and *ibi je* did do what I would *con elle* as well as I could, she *sedendo sobre* thus far and making some little resistance. But all with much content and *je tenai* much pleasure *cum ista*.' The passage is somewhat obscure. But Doll was evidently not in the mood to go to extremes that evening.

Betty Michell, however, was coming along nicely. He gave her 'two pair of gloves and a dressing-box. And so home in the dark' (he had taken his wife to the shop and they were driving Betty home) 'over the ruins' (of the late Great Fire) 'with a link. I was troubled with my pain, having got a bruise on my right testicle, I know not how. But this I did make good use of to make my wife shift sides with me and I did come to sit *avec* Betty Michell and there had her *main*, which *elle* did give me very frankly now and did *hazer* whatever I *voudrais avec la*, which did *plaisir* me *grandement* and so set her at home with my mind mighty glad of what I have prevailed for so far.' This was certainly a great advance, Mrs. Pepys being actually present at the celebrations. It is really quite extraordinary that the very jealous spouse seems to have suspected nothing. The lovers must have been exceptionally discreet and clever.

Incidentally, for some time now the French, Spanish and Latin words used in the Diary have been rather pointless. They would rarely prevent anyone with a key to the cipher from understanding the sense of the passages in which they occur. Perhaps Pepys was simply being influenced by the affected polyglot jargon used at Court and in certain learned circles, both of which he now frequented, in referring to technical or private matters. There seems little point, for example, in saying *ego ne pouvoir* instead of *I couldn't manage it* when he was simply trying to catch a glimpse of Betty. It is true, however, that when these foreign words are used the main subject is always erotic. They do not appear in the long political and business narratives.

There are a tremendous lot of them, for instance, in a longish passage which treats, with only one unprintable expression, of a complicated series of comings and goings with Betty. It may be summarised here without them and without Samuel's awkward if picturesque foggings of the issue, since it seems to prove that neither Mr. Michell nor Mrs. Pepys yet guessed what had been going on under their noses for so long.

On 11th February Samuel met Betty Michell about five in the afternoon, at the New Exchange. She asked where his wife was. He made a plausible excuse, and took the girl to a cabinet-maker's shop to buy yet another dressing-box for her. They had to wait for an hour while the thing was made. Samuel suggested a tavern but the girl declined this proposal, so they stayed in the shop to watch the box being made. The woman who owned the shop invited them into the kitchen, taking Betty for Sam's wife 'and there very merry'. At last the box was finished and they set out in the dark to drive home, enjoying themselves in the coach as usual. It then occurred to Mr. Pepys that Betty's husband might quite innocently call at the Navy Office house to see if she had been driven back there, as sometimes happened when Mrs. Pepys accompanied Samuel to the Exchange; but when he found that Mrs. P. was at home and Mr. P. absent, as he assumed, with Mrs. M., both Mr. M. and Mrs. Pepys might suspect the truth. So Samuel drove Betty straight home to her own place, where her husband was waiting for her. He told the Surveyor that he had just sent his maid to see if they had all three gone to the Navy Office house (as before). Pepys dashed off in a frenzy to catch the girl up before she could make the fatal discovery that Mrs. P. was, and had been all the time, at home. He caught her on the very steps, in the pitch dark. Luckily he recognised her voice when she enquired if this was Mr. Pepys' house; he revealed himself, told the maid that her mistress had already reached her own home and dismissed the messenger.

'But, Lord!' he continues. 'In what a trouble was I when she was gone to recollect whether this was not the second time of her coming, but at last concluding that she had not been here before, I did bless myself in my good fortune in getting home before her and do verily believe she had loitered some time by the way, which was my great good fortune, and so I in a-doors and there find all well.'

A narrow escape! Betty, too, had had a fright. A few days later, on one of the usual boat excursions with all four of the Michells 'I did to my trouble see all the way that *elle* did get as close *a su marido* as *elle* could and turn her *mains* away *quand je* did endeavour to take one . . .' (necessary gap) 'so that I had no pleasure at all *con elle ce* night. When we landed I did take occasion to send him' (i.e. the husband) 'back *a* the *bateau* while I did get a *baiser* or two and would have taken *la* by *la* hand but *elle* did turn away and *quand* I said shall I not *toucher te* answered *ego* no love touching' (the Diarist here, muddled with his foreign words, falls into pidgin English) 'in a slight' (i.e. slighting) 'mood. I seemed not to take notice of it but parted kindly; *su marido* did *aller* with me almost *a* my *case* and there we parted and I so home troubled at this but I think I shall make good use of it and mind my business more.'

She had kept close to her husband all the time, refused the former secret contacts even when alone with Pepys for a few minutes, and obviously sulked, while the husband, innocent as ever, had walked home with Samuel as usual. The last phrases probably mean rather that he was going to be extra circumspect in future than that he was going to drop the whole affair. Mr. Pepys was nothing if not as persistent in his many courtships as he was over his only slightly more multi-tudinous accounts at the office.

Mrs. Burroughs in the 'closet', i.e. Pepys' private office, and Mrs. Bagwell at Deptford were kept busy all this time by the Surveyor's attentions. On 4th March 'away to Deptford and there I a little in the yard and then to Bagwell's where I find his wife washing and also I did *hazer tout que je voudrais con* her and then sent for her husband and discoursed of his going to Harwich this week to his charge of the new ship building there which I have got him and so away . . .'

Samuel is now as much at home in the immemorial world of comic cuckoldry, with the obsequious, deceived husband arrogantly 'sent for' by the insolent lover five minutes after the latter has yet again had intercourse with the wife, as any actor since plays were first written—not forgetting peremptory instructions to the husband to absent himself in the near future, ostensibly in his own interests, on business provided for him by the seducer. To add spice to the situation Mrs. Bagwell had to participate, with what feelings may be imagined, in the interview concluding these arrangements.

Thus another husband had been efficiently disposed of, a step which, after all, had been requested by the wife herself, though at a price perhaps higher than she bargained for. But such husbands had, of course, to be kept in due order. When Martin the purser called to badger his patron for more favours, the Secretary of the Navy Board sharply intimated that he had better 'beware of coming any more with high demands for supernumeraries or other things, for . . . the passing of his accounts will not be so easy as the last. He tells me he will never need it again, it being as easy and to as much purpose to do the same thing otherwise . . .' Mr. Martin went on to say that being in charge of the catering for his vessel he was able to screw high perquisites out of his captain's profits in trade to the tune of a clear £150 per voyage of five or six months, over and above living like a fighting cock ashore. In five years' time he expected to have a capital of £1,000 to invest.

It is not quite clear whether Samuel then fell for this old confidence trick of a blackmailer, viz. the assertion that the current demand would be the last, as the petitioner would shortly be doing well from another source. Mr. Pepys certainly did not take anything like such a rosy view of the purser's prospects, and considered him a spendthrift. On the other hand Mrs. Martin was an absolute necessity to her steady lover, Samuel Pepys, and might easily make serious trouble if her husband were not kept on a satisfactory economic level, spendthrift or not, by that same Pepys. It is probable that the prudent Surveyor simply held his unwelcome visitor at bay with promises for the time being. He notes scornfully, if perhaps a little ruefully, at the end of this day (5th March): 'For my part I and my wife will keep to one another and let the world go hang, for there is nothing but falseness in it.'

Next day he was nearly caught at Mrs. Bagwell's. The carpenter's wife warned him to be off just in time. It was not Mr. Bagwell, but a mutual female friend, thought to be accompanied by one of Sam's own maids, who happened to be in the neighbourhood. 'So I away presently, esteeming it a great escape.' For a normally discreet amorist Pepys took quite a number of dangerous chances. He could afford, perhaps, to ignore gossip among the naval population along this reach of the river; if such talk came to Elizabeth's ears she would have no more proof of his delinquencies than she had from what was said by her own circle about Sam's obsessions with Mary Knipp and Mrs. Pierce. However, definite reports by his own servants, Mary Mercer or Jane, for instance, would be more difficult to refute. Still, even in the case of his own staff his unruly sexual appetite sometimes rendered him more reckless than his sober senses would have allowed. He was really getting a bit over-confident in these later years. Nevertheless, on this occasion Mrs. Bagwell's warning worked effectively. He slipped out of the trap, if it were one.

One result of Mr. Martin's new prosperity was a barrel of oysters, which his wife sent her patron this spring. The Diarist, however, received this gift with mixed feelings.

On a visit to Westminster Hall early in March 'I saw Mr. Martin, the purser, come through with a picture in his hand which he had bought and observed how all the people of the Hall did fleer and laugh upon him, crying, "There is plenty grown upon a sudden," and the truth is I was a little troubled that my favour should fall on so vain a fellow as he and the more because, me thought, the people do gaze upon me as the man that had raised him and as if they guessed whence my kindness to him springs.'

In these circumstances a visit to the couple on the 13th was not a success, 'he and she both within and with them the little widow that was once there with her when I was there, that dissembled so well to be grieved at hearing a tune that her late husband liked, but there being so much company I had no pleasure here and so away to the Hall again and there met Doll Lane coming out and *par contrat* did *hazer* bargain *para aller* to the *cabaret de vin*, called the Rose and *ibi* I staid two hours, *sed* she did not *venir, lequel* troubled me and so away by coach.' Doll, a more capricious girl than her sister, could never be relied on to keep appointments. Samuel wasted all the afternoon of the next day looking for her in vain.

As the spring came on, and the peace negotiations still hung fire, with little to do at the Navy Office until Whitehall decided whether there was to be fighting this year and if so what sort of fighting, Sir William Penn and Lord Brouncker had a furious dispute on a mere question of procedure. Then the latter accused Batten of corruption, and Minnes damned everybody heartily all round for interfering in his own sphere. Sam himself began to feel profoundly irritated with the whole lot of them. As Westminster had been so disappointing lately, and he had a little capital, he began to wonder whether he would be better off if he resigned his post and went to live in the country.

If the treaty talks broke down and the Dutch, with Louis XIV behind them, felt strong enough to invade England, life would be even less worth living in London than it was already. At Brampton in Huntingdonshire, whatever happened, he could get on with his music, take up gardening and write a history of the Navy; and no doubt there would be plenty of 'free' country girls, just the sort he liked, not expensive and no nonsense about refinement, as well as the local taverns and jolly neighbours unconcerned with politics. Perhaps it wouldn't be a bad idea.

On 23rd February this year he had written: 'This day I am by the blessing of God 34 years old, in very good health and mind's content and in condition of estate much beyond whatever my friends could expect of a child of theirs this day 34 years.' One might go further and fare worse, he could be excused for thinking, despite the promptings of an ambition by no means yet relinquished, though finding the road to glory a difficult one.

It may seem to a modern reader that thoughts of retirement were somewhat premature in the mind of this vigorous and optimistic man, young by the standards of today. He was only thirty-four. But the last few years had been pretty gruelling, well as he had done out of them financially. The plague and the fire, war work and the fearful strain of keeping on terms with half a dozen arrogant and mutually hostile lords, had really taken it out of him. His health was not quite as good as he generally pretended. In any case, as already suggested, public men in their middle thirties in the seventeenth century were more like what men nearing their fifties would be in the twentieth. If it had not been for the perpetual stream of Bettys, Dolls and Pegs who came to solace him with their kisses and *mammailles*, he might have felt even older.

As was only to be expected, it was this last consideration that in the end retained Sam at his post after all. There was no place like London for 'mirth' whether the Dutch and the French came or whether they didn't. At Brampton he would have to live with his useless brother, his boring, freckled sister, his querulous old parents and a covey of stupid, illiterate rustics. The dreariness of it would send not only him but, worse still, his temperamental wife, half crazy. They would do nothing but bicker and curse each other like the members of the Navy Board. London it must be, for a good long time yet—in fact, until the girls began to yawn at his wrinkles and grey hairs. Immediately, his meditations began to take a lewder turn.

On 24th February he had heard of Frances Tooker's venereal infection, but this intelligence did not prevent him, on 15th March, from kissing and fondling her when she unexpectedly called at his office about noon. 'Grown a little woman', he notes with calm satisfaction. Two days later, 'I would also remember to my shame how I was pleased yesterday to find the righteous' (i.e. pretty) 'maid of Magister Griffin' (the porter at the Navy Office) 'sweeping of *nostra* office'— this is an example of Pepys' unnecessary use of a Latin word— '*elle con* the Roman *nariz* and *bonne* body which I did heretofore like and do still refresh me to think *que elle* is to come to us, that I may *voir* her *aliquando*.' The maid with the Roman nose and appetising figure duly went down on his list, but only, at the moment, for pleasures of the eye.

Sarah at the Swan, Mrs. Martin and Betty Michell all came in for amorous treatment during the month. For some reason the spring had got into Samuel's anatomy this year, and he was very restless, 'my mind wandering upon *mauvaises amours*, which I be merry for . . . only out of idleness and to get some little pleasure to my *mauvais flammes*, but sped not . . .' He was unlucky, and turned to the theatre instead. But on the 24th 'I to Martin's, where I find her within and *su hermano*' (i.e. her brother, though why he should be in Spanish only the Diarist could tell us) 'and *la veuve* Burroughs. Here I did *demeurer toda* the afternoon . . .' not wasting his time either, according to the MS., here suppressed.

He heard the news of his mother's death on the 27th. On the 30th he was told that Betty Michell was pregnant. But in spite of these melancholy tidings he was again with Mrs. Martin on the 31st, and again the details of their meeting have to be omitted in the interests of decency. It is intriguing to learn that on 1st April, this experienced amorist was 'pleased with a *jolly femme* that I saw going and coming in the way, which *je* could *avoir* been contented *pour avoir* staid with if I could have gained acquaintance *con elle*, but at such times as these I am at a great loss, having not confidence, no *alcune* ready wit'. In other words, he couldn't think of anything to say to her, a rather surprising but quite characteristic confession. But he was feeling worried at the time, stating the catalogue of his woes in equally characteristic order of importance, 'that my wife's watch proves so bad as it do; the ill state of the office; the kingdom's business; and the charge which my mother's death for mourning will bring me when all paid'.

In February Peg Penn had married a man called Lowther, though she was still only fifteen; in those days girls were often married at that age, and as she was far from beautiful she could consider herself lucky, especially from one point of view, as her husband was rather stupid. On the afternoon of the 13th April she called on her old friend Samuel in his office and there '*je* did *toker ses mammailles* and did *baiser* them and *su bocca*, which she took *fort* willingly . . .' admitting certain other familiarities into the bargain.

Late that month the Dutch were sighted off the Scottish coast. Early in May their guns bombarded Burntisland, opposite Edinburgh in the Firth of Forth. So there would be no peace after all. Samuel kept calm, but he began again to think of Brampton, and warned his father that he might soon be going to retire.

Betty Michell's baby, a girl, had been born on 23rd April, just before this latest political alarm. Sam, on his way back from Mrs. Martin's, looked in to see her that same day and found mother and child both doing well. It may be conjectured that this Betty, whose 'prettiness' Sam is never tired of extolling, was dark, for his taste was so strongly in favour of brunettes that on 11th May, when his wife put on fair hair for a change,

'I was ready to burst with anger'. When she promised 'to wear white locks no more in my sight' he told her she was not to wear them at all, ever. The reproach 'made her fly out to very high terms and cry and in her heat told me of keeping company with Mrs. Knipp, saying that if I would promise never to see her more—of whom she hath more reason to suspect than I had heretofore of Pembleton—she would never wear white locks more'.

It is possible to conjecture from this passage that Samuel may by then have enjoyed the full favours of this talented actress. He was disconcerted to find that Mrs. Pepys guessed it; but he stood on his dignity and made no promises, except to himself to be more careful in future. Poor Elizabeth had to give in at last to the rights of a husband in this important matter of 'locks'.

During Betty Michell's convalescence, Mr. Pepys consoled himself with the Lanes, both the elder and the younger sister, to say nothing of little Sarah *minor* at the Swan. 'I have forgot,' he writes on 20th May, 'that I did in the morning go to the Swan and there tumbling of *la* little *fille, son* uncle did *trouver* her *cum su* neckcloth off, which I was ashamed of, but made no great matter of it, but let it pass with a laugh.' It was usually the poor maid who was blamed on these occasions. Pepys, as a frequent patron of the Swan, would naturally get off lightly when the girl's uncle accidentally caught them in this significant disarray.

On the 23rd an old friend, Mrs. Daniel, who was his landlady's daughter as well as being the wife of a naval lieutenant, called to see him. Mrs. Daniel was a frequent visitor, often dining at the house with Mr. and Mrs. Pepys; but for all that she had been well kissed and fondled by the Surveyor. Apart from her physical attractions, she was one of the many young married women who were anxious to secure Samuel's influence on behalf of their husbands.

'After dinner I to my chamber and my wife and I to talk, and by and by they tell Mrs. Daniel would speak with me, so I down to the parlour to her and sat down together and talked about getting her husband a place . . .' At this point some too explicit details of what then occurred must be omitted. 'I do promise,' he goes on, 'and mean to do what kindness I can to her husband. After having been there *hasti je* was ashamed *de peur* that my people *pensait to pragma*.' The last two words are written in Greek script. The whole of this carefully camouflaged sentence, introducing dog-Spanish and, for the second time, Greek, in addition to French, means simply that he felt worried about what the servants might think. Perhaps he thought there had been some audible hint of what was happening.

'Or lest,' he continues, 'they might espy us through some trees, we parted and I to the office and presently back home again and there was asked by my wife, I know not whether simply or with design, how I come to look as I did, *car ego* was in much *chaleur et de* body and of *animi*, which I put off with the heat of the season and so to other business, but I had some fear hung upon me lest *alcuno* had *sidi decouvert*.' He looked flustered when he returned and kept wondering whether he had been under observation. But this anxiety did not prevent further exercises of the same sort, with another partner, the very same afternoon.

'This afternoon I had opportunity *para jouer* with Mrs. Pen' (this, of course, was plain, though rich, Peg) '*tokendo* her *mammailles* and *baisando elle*, being *sola* in the *casa* of her *pater* and she *fort* willing.' Here the camouflage is thicker than ever. The Diarist puts a Spanish termination on a French word and drags in more of the former, less familiar language than usual. The sense is that the hugging and kissing took place in Sir William Penn's house, young Peg being alone there and extremely forthcoming.

Mr. Pepys had now bought a 'perspective glass' which enabled him to examine distant ladies more closely than he could with the naked eye. On the Sunday, *en route* to Mrs. Martin's, he was intercepted by Betty Michell's father, who dragged him into St. Margaret's, Westminster, to hear the sermon. For Betty's sake, he let himself be thus diverted and 'much against my will staid out the whole church in pain while she' (Mrs. Martin) 'expected me at home, but I did entertain

myself with my perspective glass up and down the church, by
which I had the great pleasure of seeing and gazing at a great
many very fine women; and what with that and sleeping I
passed away the time and then to Mrs. Martin and there staid
with her an hour or two and there did what I would with her
and after been here so long I away to my boat and up with it
as far as Barne Elmes, reading of Mr. Evelyn's late new book
against Solitude'. The unconscious humour of the last phrase
is delicious.

The title of the book he read a few days later, while repeating
the visit to Mrs. Martin followed by a solitary journey up the
river, is almost as suitable to the occasion. It was a translation
of 'The Visions' of Quevedo.

On the 28th, Sam's chivalry was aroused, and a light is cast
for his readers on contemporary manners, in Vauxhall Gardens.
'There were two pretty women alone, that walked a great
while, which being discovered by some idle gentlemen, they
would needs take them up; but to see the poor ladies, how they
were put to it to run from them, and they after them, and
sometimes the ladies put themselves along with other company,
then the other drew back; at last the last did get off out of the
house and took boat and away. I was troubled to see them
abused so; and could have found in my heart, as little desire
of fighting as I have, to have protected the ladies.'

This somewhat inelegantly expressed passage is highly
characteristic. Pepys, like many another sedulous amorist,
could not bear to watch tactics less subtle than his own,
especially if they looked like succeeding. But he would never,
as he freely confesses, carry his indignation so far as to interfere,
though interference might have furthered his own suit. He
hated disorder and squabbles, as we have more than once had
occasion to observe. Better a lost opportunity than a loss of
dignity was his motto at such times.

But much more serious affairs were very soon to claim his
attention.

8

Coping with the Bettys

O<small>N</small> 3rd June 1667, Trinity Monday, Mr. Pepys went
down to the Old Hall of Trinity House at Deptford to
see the new Master chosen. The successful candidate
turned out to be his old friend and enemy—both by turns, but
more the latter than the former—Sir William Penn. The
proceedings subsequently rather bored the Diarist. As someone
for whom he had a far greater respect, to wit his fellow-diarist
John Evelyn, was at the dinner, Sam fell into confidential talk
with him.

Evelyn said that the Dutch were out, looking for trouble,
with eighty ships of war, and that the French were in the
Channel with twenty more, 'while we have not a ship at sea
to do them any hurt with; but are calling in all we can while
our Embassadors are treating at Bredah; and the Dutch look
upon them as come to beg peace and use them accordingly;
and all this through the negligence of our Prince' (i.e. King
Charles II) 'who hath power, if he would, to master all these
with the money and men that he hath had the command of and
may now have if he would mind his business. But for aught we
see, the Kingdom is likely to be lost . . . for ever; notwithstanding so much reputation got and preserved by a rebell
that went before him.'

The 'rebell' was of course Cromwell, under whom and the
great admiral Blake English sea power had been so greatly
increased. The Surveyor was much disturbed; 'we poor and
still out of order, I know not yet what turns there may be'.
It was most annoying, as he was just thinking of buying a
coach. And if invasion was to be expected, there would be an

end to theatre-going and gay parties with the smart and not so smart sets, from Mrs. Knipp to Mrs. Martin.

On 8th June his worst fears were confirmed. The Dutch were off Harwich, and their guns had been heard at Bethnal Green. The militia were being mobilised, and everyone expected that a landing would follow. Fireships were to be despatched down the Thames. Next day the enemy ships were reported off the Nore sandbank at the very mouth of the river. On the 10th Deptford Dockyard struck for arrears of pay, and Sir William Penn had to go down and roar them into loading the fireships.

Albemarle sank frigates in the river to block it off Gravesend. By the 11th Sheerness had fallen, and Chatham was threatened. Once more Sam began to make preparations for flight into the country. He found Whitehall already half deserted of its throngs of courtiers, the taverns almost empty; worst of all, the fashionable ladies in their gorgeous coaches had abandoned the park.

By the 12th the Dutch were in the Medway, burning the ships anchored there. Samuel told Elizabeth and his father, who was staying with them, that all was lost. There might be a revolution. The family must leave for Brampton at once, though its principal member, Sam himself, could not think of going yet.

At four in the morning of the 13th he heard that the King and the Duke of York had gone down to Barking to supervise the defence measures. He immediately roused his wife and father, the latter of whom was by now a semi-invalid, gave them £1,300 in gold to bury in the garden at Brampton, and saw them off on the first coach to Huntingdon. He then packed £300 more into a body-belt next his skin, hid £400 in silver under the beds and sent his most important papers and plate for safe-keeping to cousins. That night he made a new will, leaving everything he possessed to Elizabeth and John Pepys, and had it duly copied and witnessed by his clerks, keeping one copy in his body-belt with the gold.

It is obvious from all these drastic measures that Mr. Pepys, in common with the majority of thinking men in England just then, had despaired of effective resistance to the Dutch attack. As a matter of fact, he was in a better position than most people to know how little chance there was of so corrupt, frivolous and blundering a Government—one at least of these epithets might be applied to every prominent figure at Court with the possible exception of Sir William Coventry—doing anything useful in the way of defence. It is probable that he expected London itself to fall, with a consequent end to the rising naval power which he had done so much to build up.

Yet it is most characteristic of the Diarist that he did not lose his head. He told both the Duke of York and the Duke of Albemarle that he never would. He did not. He behaved like a man of cool courage in the face of a desperate emergency. He was determined not to sacrifice his life in vain, but was ready to do so if circumstances made it impossible to escape. As a commissariat expert only, and one who had already done his full duty, it was not his concern to join in the frantic defensive steps now being taken. He turned from these tumultuous operations to see to the safety of his dependants and their inheritance if he should be so unlucky as to perish in the utter confusion which he could foresee.

No episode in his career proves so much as his conduct in June 1667 that Samuel was not simply the typical erotomaniac exhibited in so many of the entries in his Diary. He was also something much more interesting: a resolute (but not fool-hardy) citizen, an ardent (up to a point) patriot who happened to be saddled with, among other less usual attributes, an intense and permanent susceptibility to pretty feminine faces and figures. There were times when this tendency took almost complete charge of him. He complains again and again in his journal that he cannot attend to business as he ought, for think-ing of Betty Michell and literally dozens of other attractive young women, some of whom he only knew by sight. Most of them, however, were in one or other of the various stages of seduction by himself, from kissing and more or less intimate fondlings to 'doing what I would'.

These first few wild days in June did not constitute one of the periods when Pepys could not keep his mind on his work. The crisis, really a matter of life and death, with the Dutch guns thundering at his ears, gave him far too many imperative practical tasks to carry out for him to be dreaming of lips, breasts and thighs while he packed and scribbled. By the time he had made all the necessary arrangements and seen his family off to Brampton, i.e. on the 14th, serious riots, just as he had anticipated, broke out in Piccadilly and at Charing Cross.

'I do believe,' he writes that night, 'it will cost blood to answer for these miscarriages. We do not hear that the Dutch are come to Gravesend; which is a wonder.' Neither was there any news of Chatham. On the evening of the 15th the lonely husband of the charming but unpredictable Elizabeth played his flageolet 'with a heavy heart, only it pleased me to think how it may please God I may live to spend my time in the country with plainness and pleasure, though with but little glory'. We have already noticed to what pleasures in that direction he was looking forward so dubiously. As for the glory, he was ready, it seems, to bid it goodbye. Plainness alone was left; and for plainness in any sense of the word Samuel, unfortunately, had never had much taste.

But Mr. Pepys, especially with his wife absent from London, would have 'dallied' if he were going to be hanged the next morning. On 16th June, with de Ruyter's fleet still in the Medway and the entire nation on the very verge of collapse, 'did show some dalliance to my maid Nell' (this was his cook, a waterman's daughter, engaged the previous month and now retained to attend him in London) 'speaking to her of her sweetheart which she had, silly girle'. Next day, 'I have lately played the fool much with our Nell, in playing with her breasts'. On the 18th, 'did this morning dally with Nell . . .' (details follow) 'which I was afterward troubled for. To the office and there all the morning. Peg Pen come to see me and I was glad of it and did resolve to have tried her this afternoon but that there was company with *elle* at my home, whither I got her . . . to my Lady Pen's and did find occasion for Peg to go

home with me to my chamber, but there being an idle gentleman with them, he went with us and I lost my hope . . . I hear
to-day poor Michell's child is dead.'

He was indeed very depressed and distracted over public
affairs. But this condition, now that all his obligations had been
met, actually had the effect of exasperating his itch for
'dalliance'. There are further references to Nell during the
next two or three days, and on the 22nd to Mrs. Daniel, who
got a good 'towzling'. Sam was confining his amativeness to
the office and his own hearth for the moment, having no time
to go elsewhere. But on the 19th the restless Elizabeth returned,
partly out of genuine anxiety for—and jealousy of—her
equally restless consort and partly because she had once more
quarrelled with John Pepys. She told Sam that they had
mismanaged the burying of the money, doing it on a Sunday
by daylight instead of on a weekday night, when there would
be fewer people about, so that they had probably been watched.

Samuel was greatly alarmed at this ominous information,
and resolved to recover the treasure at once from its precarious
hiding-place. 'Such was my trouble at this that I fell out with
my wife, that though new come in towne I did not sup with
her nor speak to her to-night, but to bed and sleep.'

He was pretty well worn out with all this bother, and yet not
so far gone as not to repeat his 'dalliance' with Nell next day
after dinner and with Mrs. Daniel on the day after that. The
Dutch, however, had already retired, and his mind was easier.
They had not meant invasion after all. It had been merely a
raid, though a terribly costly one; immense damage had been
done to shipping in the Medway. Three battleships had been
sunk and another captured. It did not look as though Britannia
were going to rule the waves much longer. The English
commissioners at Breda were told to accept whatever terms
were offered and be quick about it.

Meanwhile, Mr. Pepys shrugged his shoulders over the
rumpus about the conduct of the war; no one could fairly
blame him for it, though some people tried to do so. After a
long inspection of the devastation caused by the recent naval

operations in the Medway the Surveyor strolled off, on the 30th, into the fields near Rochester, in company with his friend John Creed. They 'met with a young, plain, silly shopkeeper and his wife, a pretty young woman, the man's name Hawkins, and I did kiss her and we talked (and the woman of the house is a very talking, bawdy jade) and eat cherries together and then to walk in the fields till it was late and did kiss her and I believe had I had a fit time and place I might have done what I would with her . . .' He stayed with Creed at an inn that night 'merrily talking of Hawkins and his wife and troubled that Creed did see so much of my dalliance, though very little', meaning probably that the flirtation was a mild one but even so might cause Creed to gossip undesirably.

On 3rd July Mrs. Martin accused Pepys of having 'got her with child . . . and is in exceeding grief and swears that the child is mine, which I do not believe, but yet do comfort her that either it cannot be so, or if it be that I will take care to send for her husband, though I do hardly see how I can be sure of that, the ship being at sea and as far as Scotland, but however I must do it and shall find some way or other of doing it, though it do trouble me not a little'. The Surveyor was, of course, in a position to get the husband on his side in this affair. But it looked like costing money.

On the 6th, however, the day on which definite peace negotiations with the Dutch began, Mrs. Martin informed him that she had been mistaken about being pregnant. Pepys at once sent out for wine. Doll, who went to fetch the liquor, 'did come home all blubbering and swearing against one Captain Vandener, a Dutchman of the Rhenish Wine House' (evidently a renegade in the recent war) 'that pulled her into a stable by the Dog tavern and there did tumble and toss her, calling him all the rogues and toads in the world, when she knows that *elle* hath suffered me to do anything with her a hundred times'. This comment on 'a woman's falseness', as he calls it, does not do the Secretary much credit, but he was less fond of Doll, who had let him down on several occasions, than he was of her sister. Neither was he under any illusions about the younger girl's virtue when tested by others than himself.

As for the public background to Sam's private love-affairs, the King himself had never been so unpopular. He was being compared on all sides, to his disadvantage, with Louis XIV and even Cromwell. 'It is strange,' writes the Diarist, 'how he' (the Duke of York) 'and every body do now-a-days reflect upon Oliver and commend him, what brave things he did and made all the neighbour princes fear him; while here a prince come in with all the love and prayers and good liking of his people, hath lost all so soon, that it is a miracle what way a man could devise to lose so much in so little time.'

Pepys is always definitely rather prejudiced against Charles, perhaps because the fellow kept beating him at his own game of skirt-chaser, and that with an aristocratic grace and wit which the solemn Secretary could not ever quite manage. The King's virtues as a diplomat were not recognised at the time by those who were not in his secret counsels. Therefore, the general public opinion, at least according to Samuel, was in favour of revenge on the Dutch, but not while such a king as Charles remained on the throne. Meanwhile the Dutch ships patrolled the English coasts. The insolent foe seemed to be in so many places at once that rough old Batten, after being told that the Hollanders had been seen at Harwich, Portsmouth, Plymouth and Dartmouth in quick succession, banged the table and roared, 'By God! I think the Devil shits Dutchmen!'

The Devil was also providing Samuel with a lot of new pretty faces, all over the City. He eagerly took note of them at this period—and of their matrimonial situations and prospects —in the intervals of furious rows with Elizabeth, mostly on trivial subjects. He felt obliged on one such occasion to pull her nose. After this chastisement they both felt better, or at least Samuel says so.

The Duke of Buckingham was now out of the Tower, where he had been imprisoned for intriguing against Lord Clarendon, the powerful Chancellor, and was regaining his old popularity. Parliament met on 25th July, in a censorious mood, but Charles coolly adjourned them a few days later. He was waiting for ratification of the peace treaty, which he hoped would put him in a better position to bargain with his legislators.

Sam saw trouble coming, and resigned his Surveyorship. He considered it would be as well, before Parliament descended upon the Navy Office like a pack of ravening wolves, to meet them from the relatively obscure fastness of the post of Clerk of the Acts only. He could then defend himself on a reduced front. All through the rest of the summer he worked hard on the proofs of his honesty and efficiency filed at the Office.

Other evidence, that of the growing hostility between Court and Parliament, was only too clear. One of the more disgraceful incidents of this perpetual friction between powerful debauchees and administrators determined to keep up at least a show of decency was the quarrel between the Archbishop of Canterbury himself and the mad rake Sir Charles Sedley. The prelate allowed himself to point out, in a message to Sir Charles, that one of the girls Sedley had run off with lately was positively a kinswoman of the personage who now addressed him 'and did wonder that he would offer any dishonour to one' thus related to a prince of the Church. 'To which Sir Charles Sidley is said to answer "A pox take his Grace! pray tell his Grace that I believe he finds himself too old and is afraid that I should outdo him among his girls and spoil his trade." '

Pepys' informant added the remarkable postscript that 'the Archbishop is a wencher and known to be so, which is one of the most astonishing things that I have heard of . . .' It is only fair to say that there is no other testimony to his Grace's tastes in this direction, whereas Sedley had a well-deserved reputation as one of the most staggeringly impudent liars of all time. The cleric was probably quite blameless. But the atmosphere in which two such well-known public characters could exchange messages of this kind was not one calculated to keep Mr. Pepys' mind on his work and off 'wenches'.

Even his heroine Lady Castlemaine 'hath made a bishop lately, namely her uncle . . . a drunken, swearing rascal and a scandal to the Church . . .' The Secretary rightly considered that while such things were allowed it was safer to remain a humble Clerk than try for a knighthood, as he had once thought of doing, among the obstreperous followers of Charles and James.

As he toiled and listened, in mounting gloom, through these dangerous days, Mr. Pepys did not find much consolation in the high bosom of his loving wife. Their married life together had always been pretty stormy, thongh on the whole the storms had been in tea-cups, if occasionally outsize ones. But this year jealousy of the actress-singer Knipp, Nell Gwyn's friend and a really talented young woman, came to a head, though there is no absolute proof that Pepys committed adultery with her. Nell the cook was also definitely dismissed by Mrs. Pepys on 6th August. The excuse was her love of gossip and 'gadding abroad', but the real reason is not far to seek. Samuel was 'not sorry for' this decision. He had always been doubtful of the advisability of 'fouling his own nest' with the maids. As for Knipp, he dropped her for the time being in accordance with Elizabeth's wishes. There remained plenty of substitutes, from the ever-faithful Betty Martin to the easy-going, if not exactly glamorous, Peg Penn.

Mrs. Pepys anticipated her husband's usual counter-attack by keeping him solemnly informed of the dates of her menstruation, coupled with reminders that conjugal relations had not taken place for the last six months. For 'she thinks that I have some doubt that she might be with child by somebody else. Which God knows never entered into my head or whether my father observed any thing at Brampton with Coleman I know not. But I do not well to let these beginnings of dis- contents take so much root between us.' Edward Coleman was a composer and singer—and 'a rogue for women'—who also acted in stage plays. He was one of the Knipp circle, and was often at the Navy Office house. John Pepys had warned his son that Elizabeth seemed very fond of the fellow.

The Diarist did his best to reassure his hot-tempered wife. Like Byron's Childe Harold, he 'sighed for many, though he loved but one', and Mrs. Pepys was his feminine counterpart. They were really very much alike in their tantrums and reconciliations, except that Samuel's sexual appetites were much less under control and he was far more conscientious in his office work than she was as a domestic manager, though now and again she would toil really hard at reorganising their household. By 12th August, at early morning in bed, they had so far made it up that the physical particulars of their agreement must be omitted.

At once Mr. Pepys returned to his old habits, rushing to see Knipp at the theatre and uttering a rhapsody over her performance 'in her night-gowne with no lockes on but her bare face and hair only tied up in a knot behind, which is the comeliest dress that ever I saw her in to her advantage'. On the 18th, a Sunday, 'I walked towards White Hall but being wearied turned into St. Dunstan's Church, where I heard an able sermon of the minister of the place; and stood by a pretty, modest maid, whom I did labour to take by the hand and the body; but she would not, but got further and further from me; and at last I could perceive her to take pins out of her pocket to prick me if I should touch her again, which seeing I did forbear and was glad I did spy her design. And then I fell to gaze upon another pretty maid in a pew close to me and she on me; and I did go about to take her by the hand, which she suffered a little and then withdrew. So the sermon ended and the church broke up and my amours ended also and so took coach and home.'

This passage vividly illustrates both the Diarist's mentality and the manners of the day. Pepys was really interested in sermons and could be a severe critic of them. Sometimes they sent him into raptures. But his appreciation was rather of the style than of the matter. Churches all over Europe at this time and until well into the eighteenth century were regularly frequented for reasons which had nothing to do with piety. For it was there, even more than at the theatre, that the amorously inclined of a particular district could take stock of one another, scrape acquaintance and make appointments, the solemnity of the place and the devotion of the more strait-laced of the congregation facilitating these secret exchanges. A respectable woman could not be accosted elsewhere without feeling it her duty to protest, in case neighbours were watching; but in church, as the above passage indicates, most people would be looking the other way. Moreover, the adventurous male would not have to fear an outcry in the sacred precincts. At worst he would note such a threatening gesture as Mr. Pepys observed on this occasion. The withdrawal of the second girl's hand probably meant that she had repented for some good reason of her earlier indiscretion. So he did not pursue the matter. But no doubt he considered it a pleasant interlude.

On the 21st 'to Westminster Hall and there staid a while and thence to Mrs. Martin's and there did take a little pleasure, both with her and her sister. Here sat and talked and it is a strange thing to see the impudence of the woman that desires by all means to have her *mari* come home only that she might be at liberty to have me *para toker* her which is a thing I do not so much desire.' It is not very clear why Betty Martin should feel more 'at liberty' with her husband at home. The Diarist seems to suggest that his presence would add spice to their arrangements from her point of view, though by no means from his. Perhaps she wanted to show Martin how popular she was with fine gentlemen. The *mari*, in any case, was outrageously *complaisant*, and possibly the wife enjoyed humiliating him with scenes which he may himself have been base enough to enjoy, *à la* Sacher-Masoch.

With Betty Michell, after her recent sad experiences, Samuel had to start all over again. On 7th September 'in the afternoon I walked to the Old Swan, the way mighty dirty, and there called at Michell's and there had opportunity *para* kiss *su moher*' (for *mujer*, Spanish for wife) 'but *elle* did receive it with a great deal of seeming regret, which did vex me. But however I do not doubt overcoming her as I did the *moher* of the *monsieur* at Deptford.' For once, however, optimistic Sam was wrong in his expectation. The usual meeting with Betty Martin followed. Of the two Bettys, Mrs. Michell was much the more respectable. She seems to have been genuinely fond of her usually decent young husband, and Mr. Pepys' remorseless pursuit of her shows him at his most callous.

On the whole, however, Samuel was far more sensitive in human relationships than most of the men or even women of his day. Of the latter Barbara Castlemaine in particular, whom the Diarist solemnly worshipped from afar, showed practically no ordinary sympathy or affection for anyone at all, not even her royal lover, throughout her fairly long life—she lived to be sixty-nine, after prosecuting her last husband for bigamy. The outspoken and truthful Comte de Gramont, in his memoirs of Charles' Court, where he spent two years in exile from Paris, describes Lady Castlemaine as 'disagreeable from the un-polished state of her manners, her ill-timed pride, her uneven temper and extravagant humours'.

Both Clarendon's fall—which occurred this autumn—and Buckingham's rise were accompanied by some picturesque antics of this notorious creature, the Diarist's 'ideal'. Her termagant beauty always fascinated Samuel, even to the extent of having a picture of her in his house. Elizabeth, for once, was not jealous, for it was as difficult for her to imagine Sam in the Castlemaine's arms as it was easy for him to imagine that he was. The case was one, rare with Mr. Pepys, of adoration at a necessarily respectful distance. He had never even spoken to Lady Castlemaine, but he lapped up every scrap of gossip he could hear about her as eagerly as any modern reader of a popular Sunday newspaper. There were a great many scraps, mostly discreditable, for obvious reasons; but Sam loved them all, and relates a few with considerable gusto.

Charles had shown some resolution during the Dutch raid, but he was rather like the Secretary himself in his rapid changes from courage and industry to utterly irresponsible frivolity. It was said that while de Ruyter was burning the English fleet off Rochester and Chatham his Majesty was at supper with the Duchess of Monmouth and Lady Castlemaine, 'hunting a moth' with extreme enthusiasm and shrieks of laughter.

The Duke of Buckingham, who had been ordered to the

Tower for treason in March 1667, was a wild but able fellow according to John Dryden, Pepys' contemporary:

> '*A man so various that he seemed to be*
> *not one but all mankind's epitome;*
> *stiff in opinions, always in the wrong;*
> *was everything by starts and nothing long,*
> *but in the course of one revolving moon*
> *was chymist, fiddler, statesman and buffoon;*
> *then all for women, painting, rhyming, drinking,*
> *besides ten thousand freaks that died in thinking.*'

The King liked Buckingham, and so did Lady Castlemaine; but it would have been very impolitic to release him at a certain moment when 'Barbary', as Charles always called her, imperiously demanded that the Duke be set at liberty. The monarch and his mistress had a full-scale slanging match over the question. 'Don't be a fool,' said Charles. 'You're interfering in a matter which has nothing to do with you.' 'You're an idiot,' cried the lady. 'If you weren't, you wouldn't let your business be conducted by imbeciles who know nothing about it and send your most loyal subjects to prison.' She meant Clarendon, whom she hated, and Buckingham, whom at the moment she adored. In the end, as usual, she won the day, as she also did about the same time, when the King swore he would not recognise the child of whom she was then pregnant. 'God damn me, you shall own it,' screamed Barbary, like any fishwife; 'I'll have it christened in the Chapel at Whitehall, or I'll bring it into the gallery and dash its brains out before your face!' She made the King of England ask her pardon on his knees.

Another story was about Clarendon's dismissal. 'Pierce, the surgeon, tells me how this business of my Lord Chancellor's was certainly designed in my Lady Castlemayne's chamber; and that when he went from the King on Monday morning' (26th August) 'she was in bed, though about twelve o'clock, and ran out in her smock into her aviary looking into White Hall garden; and thither her woman brought her her nightgown; and stood joying herself at the old man's going away: and several of the gallants of White Hall, of which there were many staying to see the Chancellor's return, did talk to her in her birdcage . . . telling her she was the bird of paradise.'

Samuel makes no comment on this somewhat sordid behaviour of his heroine, as she exulted in the disgrace of her aged enemy. The truth is, undoubtedly, that Barbary's heart and soul were not quite up to the mark of her face and figure. In fact, her vindictive cruelty, fatuous conceit and shallowness, to say nothing of her frequent raging tempers and foul manners, would have frightened and disgusted the good Samuel out of his wits if his many fantasies about lying with her had ever come true. Yet her beauty and high spirits made up for all in the views of many more sceptical amorists than Mr. Pepys. The magnificence of her appearance, like great poetry written by a squalid sponger, made everyone forget, at least from time to time, what lay, or rather crawled, behind it.

By 1667 the infatuated Diarist could not so easily 'glut himself with looking at her'. She was as lovely as ever. The only trouble was that Mr. Pepys' eyes had now been failing him for some time, and there are more and more numerous remarks on this subject in the Diary. He certainly used his sight more than most men of his day, whether in gazing upon 'visions' of pretty women, poring over his accounts, staring at the theatre with the critical scrutiny of an almost professional playgoer, reading and writing notes of music or straining his eyes under flickering candles over a great many small and ill-printed books late at night, or even examining series of engravings, not to mention what was perhaps the worst trial of all, the composition in crabbed cipher of the immortal journal. He was to go nearly blind in the end, or we should have had more of the Diary. A certain occasional acerbity of tone in Mr. Pepys' literary style is no doubt partly to be referred to this condition, together with a growing general cynicism in his dealings with Betty Michell and others of his lady-loves.

9

Road to Glory

AT the end of September another change of domestic staff took place. It was an interesting one, so interesting that it almost looks as if Mrs. Pepys were laying a trap for her susceptible husband. 'While I was busy at the office my wife sends for me to come home and what was it but to see the pretty girl which she is taking to wait upon her: and though she seems not altogether so great a beauty as she had before told me, yet indeed she is mighty pretty; and so pretty that I find I shall be too much pleased with it, and therefore could be contented as to my judgement, though not to my passion, that she might not come, lest I may be found too much minding her, to the discontent of my wife. She is to come next week. She seems by her discourse to be grave beyond her bigness and age and exceeding well bred as to her deportment, having been a scholar in a school at Bow these seven or eight years. To the office again, my head running on this pretty girl . . .'

The Secretary had reached a point in his amorous and conjugal career when a fresh encounter induced about equal measures of delight and terror in him. He could no more resist a new pretty face than he could resist a new song, a new play or a further complication in his accounts. Yet by this time, his sexual susceptibilities had really begun to menace one of the main props of his succes in life, the maintenance of Elizabeth's affections; the challenge had to be met. There was no question of retreating before it.

That day, to his further satisfaction, he heard good news of his patron, Lord Sandwich. The earl, now aggressively bearded in the Spanish manner, had concluded an excellent treaty with the country to which he was accredited. The City was delighted with it, the commercial terms being very favourable, and the King had it printed and published at once, before ratification. This was the first public act for several years that met with the Diarist's approval. In his opinion Charles's reign, after a promising start, had been a record of one disaster after another, including Lord Sandwich's own loss of prestige in the ill-advised distribution of the prize cargoes taken in 1665.

The earl himself was not avaricious. In fact, he was aristocratically careless about money, and therefore regularly in need of it. His family sometimes applied to Pepys for loans, which that astute gentleman was very unwilling to grant, much as he loved his patron, for he knew that it would be difficult to recover his money. Consequently, the tidings that Sandwich's very real abilities, in diplomacy as in naval warfare, had again been rewarded greatly pleased the Diarist.

So the autumn had started well. As regards the new maid, he was especially gratified that Elizabeth seemed to think highly of her. The fact promised a clear field for preliminary negotiations, at any rate. As a rule his wife was in the habit of expressing a certain pessimism, as well as extreme vigilance, every time they replaced female staff; but this time she showed neither the one nor the other. Mr. Pepys discreetly agreed with everything Mrs. Pepys said, and bided his time.

While awaiting the arrival of this latest paragon, he went into training, so to speak, with Sarah at the Swan and Mrs. Martin, to the latter of whom, after 'having all with her', he was unusually generous, offering to pay for her little daughter's first 'coat'. When the new girl, whose name was Willet, eventually showed up for duty, Sam could hardly take his eyes off her. 'She is very pretty and so grave as I never saw a little thing in my life. Indeed I think her a little too good for my family and so well carriaged as I hardly ever saw. I wish my wife may use her well.' He proceeded to spend quite a lot of time with the two of them together, at the theatre and on various shopping and other excursions.

Of course, he still had time for Betty Martin. On 4th October

'I to Westminster, to Mrs. Martin's lodging, whither I sent for her, and there hear that her husband is come from sea, which is sooner than I expected; and here I staid and drank, and so did *toucher elle* and away . . .' As usual, the purser's returns to the arms of his all too loving consort coincided with a brusque intensification of Sam's own attentions to the lady, with whom, nevertheless, he seldom wasted more time than was absolutely necessary to note the lie of the land and ensure his own 'pleasure'.

That same day he heard that Sir William Batten, his tough old colleague on the Navy Board, had suddenly fallen ill, so seriously that he was not expected to live. The news, Samuel characteristically adds, 'troubles me and my wife mightily, partly out of kindness . . . and partly because of the money he owes me . . .' Batten died the next day. The nature of his illness is not specified, but people often died unexpectedly in those days of careless living and weird medical remedies. Pepys had always considered this veteran seaman and ranker knight as a bit of a rogue, by no means above 'knavery' and underhand dealing, but as a rule he got on well enough with him, since the two had at least the virtues of patriotism and courage in common.

Mrs. Pepys was charmed by her husband's new generosity to her and Willet in the shops. It arose of course from his interest in the maid, 'which I dare not own', but at this period Elizabeth does not seem to have suspected the existence of this feeling. No doubt he concealed it under a special show of indifference. She did not even mind when at the King's theatre the three of them 'met with Knepp and she took us up into the tireing-rooms: and to the women's shift, where Nell' (Nell Gwyn) 'was dressing herself and was all unready and is very pretty, prettier than I thought. And so walked all up and down the house above and then below into the scene-room and there sat down and she gave us fruit: and here I read the questions to Knepp' (i.e. rehearsed her).

'But, Lord!' he adds with characteristic primness, 'to see how they were both painted would make a man mad and did make me loath them; and what base company of men comes among them and how lewdly they talk and how poor the men are in clothes and yet what a shew they make on the stage by candle-light is very observable. But to see how Nell cursed, for having so few people in the pit, was pretty . . .'

On 7th October Mr. and Mrs. Pepys, with Willet and several friends, including Peg Penn and her husband, set out on a week's tour through the shires of Huntingdon and Cambridge. The Pepys couple and their maid stayed the first night at the 'Raynedeere', a tavern in Bishops Stortford, where the hostess, one Mrs. Aynsworth, was an old friend of Sam's from his Cambridge days. 'I knew her,' he remarks complacently, 'better than they think for.' Recalling his relatively innocent diversions as an undergraduate, he goes on: 'It was the woman that, among other things, was great with my cozen Barnston of Cottenham and did use to sing to him and did teach me "Full forty times over", a very lewd song . . . she is here what she was at Cambridge and all the good fellows of the country come hither.'

Elizabeth Aynsworth is known from other sources to have been a highly popular procuress at Cambridge in Pepys' time. She was eventually expelled by the university authorities, whom she nevertheless 'nobly' entertained at the Reindeer subsequently, telling the Vice-Chancellor, who was one of them, that she would not dream of charging him for her hospitality, since he had made her fortune by driving her out of Cambridge. The local gentlemen evidently paid up more handsomely than the undergraduates had.

Only about a month before Sam's arrival at the Reindeer with his wife and maid, Mrs. Aynsworth had been tried at Chelmsford as an accessory before the fact of the murder of Captain Wood of Hertfordshire at a place called Manuden in Essex. She was acquitted for want of evidence, but not before she had tried to throw herself into the river on the way to prison. One Boteler was hanged for the murder on 10th September. There is a flavour of the Wild West about this typical Restoration story; if more details were known it might make a good film.

At the Reindeer, 'my wife and I in one bed and the girl in another, in the same room, and lay very well, but there was so much tearing company in the house that we could not see my landlady; so I had no opportunity of renewing my old acquaintance with her, but here we slept very well'. Mrs. Aynsworth knew better than many a more respectable woman how to look after her guests. Neither did her riotous local clients worry the party from London in the least.

At Cambridge they had similar accommodation, the three of them in one room, a usual enough custom at the time, 'very merry talking together and mightily pleased both of us with the girl'. It is significant, however, that this time Sam slept in one bed and Mrs. Pepys and the maid in the other, thus preventing any conceivable night-wandering by the husband.

They went on to pay a visit to John Pepys at Brampton. Here Elizabeth, as usual, put on airs. 'My father tells me that he is troubled that my wife shows my sister no countenance and him but very little, but is as a stranger in the house; and I do observe she do carry herself very high; but I perceive there was some great falling out when she was here last, but the reason I have no mind to enquire after, for vexing myself, being desirous to pass my time with as much mirth as I can while I am abroad.'

It is probable that John Pepys, an honest but not over-intelligent old fellow, had thought Elizabeth's flirtatious London manners improper in the absence of her husband, and had bluntly told her so. Nothing could be more calculated to send her rocketing into a passion. Sam's dull and ugly sister Pall (Paulina) may have added her own jealous gossip. It was no doubt an example of the common case of humdrum people disliking the sharp-tongued gaiety of an intruder by marriage into the family circle, believing it to be something worse and making no secret of their belief. It is very unlikely that the shrewd, if often recklessly vivacious and aggressive, Elizabeth took any chances on her grass widow's holidays at Brampton which might cause trouble with Samuel. Neither does it seem that he ever seriously suspected her of doing so, though he is occasionally a little uneasy on the subject.

The three visitors stayed that night in one room together at the Brampton house, with Willet in a 'trundle' bed, i.e. a low bedstead on wheels, which was run in under the big bed in which the married couple slept. Here again it is possible to see a deliberate disposition on the part of Mrs. Pepys. They decided to stay at Brampton another day. That evening Sam was up half the night digging in the garden for the gold he had sent to his father to hide when the Dutch were in the Medway. Coming late to bed, he found Elizabeth and the girl already snoring in the big bed and had to make do with the 'trundle'. 'I lay in some disquiet all night,' thinking less of Willet, however, than of having been unable to find some fifty pieces of the gold coin which had been buried. Only about six inches of earth had covered the rotted box containing the money. The sacks, also rotted, came to pieces when he tried to pull them out, and the coins rolled about in the dark. By two in the morning both he and Will Hewer, who was helping him to search with a dark lantern, were exhausted, and a number of the coins were still missing.

They slept for three hours, and then went back to work. Four hours later they had recovered more of the money and repacked it, with the exception of some twenty or thirty pieces. Mr. Pepys, who had lost his temper the night before, regained it in considering that the missing sum was not great in comparison with the desperate emergency which had led to it. It 'gives me some kind of content to remember how painful it is sometimes to keep money, as well as to get it . . .' he sagely observes.

At about ten o'clock that morning, the 11th, the party, reinforced by Sam's brother John and a servant borrowed from Lady Sandwich's house in the neighbourhood, set off for London, with the gold in a basket under one of the seats in the coach. Samuel was in a fever of apprehension of highwaymen all the way, but after a night at Stevenage they reached

London safely. On the whole the expedition had been successful and very enjoyable; but Mrs. Pepys 'I perceive is already a little jealous of my being fond of Willet, but I will avoid giving her any cause to continue in that mind as much as possible'. The phrase is non-committal, indicating that he considered the field still open, if negotiated with prudence. The Secretary was an incurable optimist.

A short revel with the two Lanes and Mrs. Burroughs followed on 13th October. Next day he was again with Mrs. Martin 'where by appointment comes to me Mrs. Howlett' (Betty Michell's mother) 'which I was afraid was to have told me something of my freedom with her daughter, but it was not so, but only to complain to me of her son-in-law, how he abuses and makes a slave of her' (Betty, presumably) 'and his mother is one that encourages him in it, so that they are at this time upon very bad terms one with another, and desires that I would take a time to advise him and tell him what it becomes him to do, which office I am very glad of, for some ends of my own also *con sa fille* and there drank and parted, I mightily satisfied with this business . . .'

As we know, Betty had been somewhat stand-offish lately and Sam had been racking his brains to think of some way of bringing her to heel. To give the husband a sharp lecture and thus earn her gratitude would be an excellent means of renewing their former intimacies.

At the theatre on the 15th, however, the busy generalissimo of 'amours' received a check in another part of the extensive area of his operations. 'Before the play begun my wife begun to complain to me of Willet's confidence in sitting cheek by jowl by us' (maids accompanying their employers to the theatre were really supposed to sit elsewhere) 'which was a poor thing' (Pepys, with characteristic charity, means that he thought the custom absurd) 'but I perceive she is already jealous of my kindness to her, so that I begin to fear this girle is not likely to stay long with us.'

Parliament had already reassembled, and was intent on finding scapegoats to blame for the disastrous outcome of the late war with the Dutch. A committee, called the Committee of Miscarriages, was appointed to hear evidence and investigate charges of corruption, negligence and mistaken action. Samuel promptly supplied the Committee with all the information it asked for, and assured it of the loyal co-operation of his Office. 'I hear everybody speaks of me,' he writes on 20th October. 'And indeed I think without vanity I may expect to be profited rather than injured by this inquiry . . .'

All through the last half of this month he was extremely busy with defending the Navy office against the charges made by Parliament of mismanagement of the recent hostilities. He succeeded in proving that the blame lay elsewhere and that he was himself, incidentally, a model official, master of every detail of his intricate work, ingenious, resolute, tireless and remarkably honest. This feat made him greatly respected in administrative circles and particularly impressed the Duke of York. He had not time to see to Betty Michell until the 31st, when 'calling at Michell's saw and once kissed *su* wife, but I do think that he is jealous of her and so she dares not stand out of his sight; so could not do more . . .' He tactfully asked the couple to dinner on 10th November, but what with pressure of business and failing sight the 'amours' made little progress for the rest of the month.

On 23rd October he had tipped Betty Martin no less than £3 'to buy my goddaughter her first new gowne . . .' This largesse indicates the Diarist's new optimism and confidence in his professional prospects, which were in fact beginning to be quite glorious. He felt himself to be a pillar of admired rectitude among toppling reputations and angry recriminations. 'I am in great fear of nothing but the damned business of the prizes, but I fear my Lord' (Sandwich) 'will receive a cursed deal of trouble by it.'

On the 26th Dr. and Mrs. Pierce dined with him. The lady told him a good story of a row between Nell Gwyn and another actress named Beck Marshall, daughter of a pious Presbyterian, when the latter called Nelly 'my Lord Buckhurst's whore'. This peer, a debauched man of letters and crony of the notorious rake Sir Charles Sedley, had been keeping Nell at Epsom ever since the previous year. She screamed back at her antagonist: 'I was but one man's whore, though I was brought up in a bawdy-house to fill strong waters to the guests; and you are a whore to three or four, though a Presbyter's praying daughter!' Nell Gwyn could hold her own anywhere, with anyone, except when she was asked to play serious parts on the stage.

Sam, after recording his entire approval of this anecdote, adds: 'Mrs. Pierce is still very pretty, but paints red on her face, which makes me hate her, that I thank God I take no pleasure in her at all more'—as commanded, he might also have added, by Elizabeth. For once he kept his word, being the kind of hearty lover who does not care for the taste of rouge. Moreover, he now had an absolute foil to the highly sophisticated Mrs. Pierce in the unadorned shape of that pretty little innocent, the maid Willet. He was never really more than dazzled by fine ladies. It was always girls of a slightly lower social station than his own who made most appeal to his intimate feelings. A few days later he contemptuously censures a certain Sir John Chichly for 'foolish talk of ladies and love and I know not what'.

The excuse of _his_ failing sight—he now regularly wore spectacles at work—enabled him at last to initiate some cautious preliminary 'dalliance' with Willet. He got into a regular habit of calling her to comb his hair before he undressed for bed, so that he could sit back, close his eyes and lose himself in a dream of closer contacts. Occasionally she could not help a light, accidental pressure of her limbs or body against his. Even the intervening garments did not detract from the keen excitement of these experiences. Often they took place in the presence of his wife, who would read to him at the same time.

But during the day he was fully occupied, as a rule, with the important business of the Committee of Miscarriages. His whole career depended on his making no mistake in dealing with it, and there was a tremendous lot of tedious collection of testimony and involved explanation to be done in connection with it. The Duke of York had told him not to hesitate in his self-defence, even if it meant apologising for some of his colleagues.

All the same, after about a month of this slavery, he felt he could allow himself an interlude or two. On 4th December, on entering the House of Commons: 'there spied a pretty woman with spots' (i.e. the fashionable black patches) 'on her face, well clad, who was enquiring for the guard chamber; I followed her and there she went up and turned into the turning towards the chapel and I after her and upon the stairs there met her coming up again and there kissed her twice and her business was to enquire for Sir Edward Bishop, one of the serjeants-at-armes. I believe she was a woman of pleasure, but was shy enough to me . . .'

This encounter, though trivial enough, reminded the Diarist that he, too, was a man of pleasure. There and then 'I to Westminster Hall and . . . spying Mrs. Burroughs in a shop did stop . . . but was upon business and I could not get her to go any whither . . .' On the 7th 'while we were at dinner comes Willet's aunt to see her and my wife; she is a fine widow and pretty handsome, but extraordinarily well carriaged and speaks very handsomely and with extraordinary understanding, so as I spent the whole afternoon in her company with my wife, she understanding all the things of note touching plays and fashions and Court and everything and speaks rarely which pleases me mightily and seems to love her niece very well and was so glad (which was pretty odde) that since she came hither her breasts begin to swell, she being afeard before that she would have none, which was a pretty kind of content she gave herself'.

From this passage it seems likely that Willet was very young, as well as very well behaved, the combination probably partly accounting for the Diarist's unwonted timidity in getting to work on her, though of course his wife's jealousy, his eye-strain and his mental exhaustion in the then condition of public affairs had a great deal to do with it.

Parliament adjourned on the 19th December, after bringing in a bill of indictment for treason against Lord Clarendon, who at once went into exile in France, and another for the investigation of the accounts kept by all officers concerned with the expenditure of public funds during the recent war. The House was to meet again on 6th February 1668.

Mr. Pepys felt a little freer to consider his private life, though there would still be much to do before Parliament returned to the charge. On Sunday the 22nd, he gained a little ground with Willet: 'Down to my chamber to settle some papers and thither come to me Willet with an errand from her mistress and this time I first did give her a little kiss, she being a very pretty humoured girle and so one that I do love mightily.' The tone is as tenderly sentimental as it was originally with Betty Michell and very different from that which Pepys adopts in other connections, that of Doll Lane for instance, or Peg Penn. Like every true amorist, the Diarist was capable of many different manners. In fact, Betty Michell and Willet seem to a modern judgment to have been the most attractive of his many loves.

At Court the only comparable figure at this time, though a controversial one, was Lady Castlemaine's great rival, Frances Stuart, now Duchess of Richmond. Before her marriage this interesting lady had laughed at the pompous Earl of Arlington for giving her advice as to how to behave when she became the King's mistress. She had less personality, but better manners than 'Barbary'. The Comte de Gramont notes that 'she was childish in her behaviour and laughed at everything and her taste for frivolous amusements, though unaffected, was only allowable in a girl about twelve or thirteen years old . . . blind man's buff was her most favourite amusement . . .' and building houses of cards, while others fervently gambled, came second.

Pepys believed she really did become the King's mistress in 1663, but Evelyn told him in 1667 that she had been virtuous until her marriage—which took place early in that year, and annoyed Charles very much. It is possible that by that time

Frances had realised that she could never permanently oust
Barbara Castlemaine from the King's favour. Richmond was a
drunken nonentity, but nobody else dared to risk Charles's
displeasure, and Lady Castlemaine was making her rival's life
impossible. Probably most of the scandal about Frances was
started by 'Barbary'; but whether chaste or not the future
Duchess of Richmond certainly had more charm, as well as
better legs, than most of the Maids of Honour.

On 26th December 1667 Pepys heard that the Duchess kept
a 'great Court' with her husband, 'she being visited for her
beauty's sake by people, as the Queen is, at nights; and they
say also that she is likely to go to Court again and there put
my Lady Castlemayne's nose out of joynt. God knows that
would make a great turn.' She was 'sworn of the Queen's
Bedchamber' some six months later. But we do not hear that
Lady Castlemaine made any great fuss about it, only that the
two ladies 'were strange to one another'.

As usual, there was much 'merriment' in London after
Christmas. On the 28th 'I rose soon from dinner and with my
wife and girle—' (so the Diarist has been calling the magnetic
little Willet for some time now)—'to the King's house' (i.e.
theatre) 'and there saw *The Mad Couple*, which is but an
ordinary play; but only Nell's and Hart's mad parts are most
excellently done, but especially hers'. The popular comedian
Charles Hart, a great-nephew of Shakespeare, was supposed to
have been Nell's first lover, or 'Charles I', as the wits put it.
He became one of the many lovers of Lady Castlemaine in the
following year, when the King was exceptionally busy with
the dancer-actress Moll Davis.

'It pleased us mightily,' Mr. Pepys continues, 'to see the
natural affection of a poor woman, the mother of one of the
children brought on the stage: the child crying, she by force
got upon the stage and took up her child and carried it away
off of the stage from Hart.' Anything might happen among the
impulsive audience at a Restoration play in those carefree days.
If anyone had tried to stop the indignant mother the cheering
spectators would probably have lynched him. The sadness

with which the English began to take their pleasures in the nineteenth century had by no means started in the seventeenth. Charles II's Londoners would have boycotted any theatre management which insisted on calm behaviour by those who had paid to enjoy themselves.

The year ended with another scene between husband and wife about Mary Knipp or Knepp—the name is variously spelt in the Diary and everywhere else—because Pepys had been to the theatre with the actress, and had heard her sing in a friend's house later. Elizabeth 'was as mad as a devil and nothing but ill words between us all the evening while we sat at cards— W. Hewer and the girl by—even to gross ill words, which I was troubled for'. He weathered this fearful storm by simply holding his tongue, an expedient which generally worked. After years of marriage, Mrs. Pepys' temper was certainly not improving, but on this occasion she may have deliberately meant to make Sam look a rascal in front of little Mistress Willet, to prevent the girl listening to any possible future declarations from him. If so, it is not at all certain that she succeeded, as we shall see.

On the 31st, too, there was an unpleasant dispute with Mrs. Martin, with whom Samuel found fault—after '*hazer con elle* what I desired'—for 'her husband's wearing of too fine clothes, by which I perceive he will be a beggar'. This puritanical lecture by the originator of a somewhat worthless family's rise in the world, which he had engineered simply in order to 'do what he would' with the wife, casts an amusing sidelight upon the complexities of the Secretary's character. He was far more shocked by the theoretically injured but practically benefited husband's naïve ostentation than by the adulterous liaison which had brought it about.

In the New Year he begins to refer to Willet as 'Deb' in the journal, her Christian name, apparently, being Deborah. 'By the fireside to have my head combed, as I do now often do, by Deb, whom I love should be fiddling about me.' He was so fond of this innocent amusement that he sometimes positively fell asleep while it was going on. Though he was not yet forty, times had changed for Mr. Pepys since he had regularly taken this opportunity to proceed to familiarities with the operator. He was beginning to treat Deb more like a daughter than a prospective mistress. He was of course childless, and often regretted it.

On 6th February, after a merry evening at the theatre, with a supper afterwards and a long drive home, the coachman having lost the way, 'I did put my hand under the coats of Mercer and did touch her thigh, but then she did put by my hand and no hurt done, but talked and sang and was merry'. Mary Mercer had of course been in Pepys' service for a good long time, ever since September 1664, and was used to the occasional liberties he took with her. It does not appear from the Diary that he ever went far in this connection. The casual contact here referred to was only a minor 'frolique', received as such.

About a month before this date he had seen at his bookseller's 'L'Escole des Filles' by a man named Helot, 'the most bawdy, lewd book that ever I saw . . . so that I was ashamed of reading in it . . .' He returned to the shop on 8th February and after hesitating an hour bought this 'idle, rogueish book . . . which I have bought in plain binding, avoiding the buying of it better bound, because I have resolved, as soon as I have read it, to burn it, that it may not stand in the list of books, nor among them, to disgrace them if it should be found'. Four years later 'L'Escole des Filles' was burnt at the foot of the gallows and the author himself was burnt in effigy. It was too much even for the age of Louis XIV. But on looking further into it the next day Pepys remarks: '. . . a mighty lewd book, but yet not amiss for a sober man once to read over to inform himself in the villainy of the world.' Such has always been the apology of those who purchase pornography and yet insist on being regarded as respectable. Nor is this defence either so feeble or invariably so hypocritical as is often supposed. The Diarist's actual motive, at any rate, in making this temporary addition to his library, was probably fifty per cent natural prurience and fifty per cent genuine curiosity about human nature.

He read through the whole thing that night, repeated the verdict already quoted and duly burnt the book as he had intended.

This spring was a trying time for Samuel. In spite of the satisfactory statement he had made the previous year to the Parliamentary Committee of Inquiry into Miscarriages in the War, he was continually being summoned to answer further charges 'which makes me mad, that I should by my place become the hackney of this Office, in perpetual trouble and vexation . . . my head being split almost with the variety of troubles upon me at this time . . .' Moreover, for some reason Betty Michell was still keeping out of his way, though he continued on the best of terms with her husband and parents. On 1st March he saw Mrs. Martin 'where I have not been also a good while', but only managed to get her to himself with some difficulty, as she had 'company'.

He was now called upon to defend the Navy at the bar of the House of Commons, 'never in so much trouble in all my life of mind, thinking of the task I have upon me and upon what dissatisfactory grounds and what the issue of it may be to me', so that he resolved 'to quit my hands of this Office and endure the trouble of it no longer than I can clear myself of it'.

Just before noon on the 5th he began his speech to the House. It lasted without a break until past three o'clock. His colleagues congratulated him heartily when he had finished. He had in fact made out his case with great skill. No further proceedings were taken in Parliament on the subject. Samuel Pepys, whatever else might be said about him, had proved himself as cool, brilliant and honest a Civil Servant as ever advised a Minister. These are qualities not commonly found in a Don Juan, serviceable as they sometimes are in the Courts of Love—as Sam himself showed more than once in his dealings with his spitfire wife and also with some of his unofficial female partners, equally 'difficult' on occasion.

He was told he would make a good Chancery lawyer, and

was complimented by the Solicitor-General himself. The King, the Duke of York and the whole Court praised him to his face. It is greatly to Sam's credit that, though naturally elated by all this unexpected glory, he did not lose his head, but continued to live as modestly as before—in the economic if not in the sexual sense.

10

Waning Daylight

THE Secretary of the Navy Board had saved the credit of
the Fleet. The Parliamentary Commissioners of Account
refrained from passing a vote of censure, and a substantial sum was allotted for the future defence of the realm.
But Samuel's most powerful patron, the Catholic Duke of
York, had to meet the hostility of the rising star of the Duke of
Buckingham, the King's current favourite, a Parliament man,
a declared Protestant and champion of the City merchants.

Meanwhile Betty Michell continued to keep the Secretary at
bay, despite his new fame. This virtuous procedure was
undoubtedly much to her credit. Unfortunately, from Sam's
point of view, Mr. Michell did not need his assistance so much
as Mr. Bagwell or Mr. Martin did; and it is of course a truism
that success in the economic field—or for that matter in any
field which has nothing to do with love-making—does not
necessarily mean a corresponding advance in the invasion of a
girl's heart, particularly if the girl concerned is a respectable
young housewife. Mr. Pepys, perhaps, was making this
discovery for the first time, much to his chagrin.

However, the other Betty, Mrs. Martin, her sister Doll and
Mrs. Burroughs consoled him. Little Mrs. Daniel also remained
on call. Deb Willet was not in this category yet, but late on the
night of 31st March 'I called Deb to take pen, ink and paper
and write down what things come into my head for my wife
to do in order to her going into the country, and the girl,
writing not so well as she would do, cried, and her mistress
construed it to be sullenness and so' (he) 'away angry with her

too, but going to bed she' (Deb) 'undressed me and there I did give her good advice and *baiser la, elle* weeping still'.

The prudent hunter of little Deb's virginity felt bound, in his wife's presence, to support the latter's somewhat tyrannical persecution of the girl on this occasion. The victim, poor child, was probably simply tired out; after all, it was late at night. In this passage, however, French words are used for the first time in relation to Deborah, indicating that her master had now ceased to regard her as his daughter—if indeed he had ever really done so. Next morning, after 'call as I use Deb to brush and dress me . . .' he adds some details which leave no doubt of his thoroughly unparental feelings towards her. As Mrs. Pepys was about to leave for Brampton, the time for a general acceleration of 'amours' seemed about ripe. Unfortunately Deb was going with her, so Sam contented himself with a farewell kiss on the girl's lips and a gift of ten shillings 'to oblige her to please her mistress', since he was now very anxious for Deb to remain in his service. Elizabeth was apt to have rows with her maids on these visits.

Contrary to Mr. Pepys' usual practice, for some days after the departure of his wife and Deb for the country, he did not go a-roving. He was pretty busy at the Office and perhaps also still thinking of that wonderful little 'girle', Willet, and wondering how she was getting on with Elizabeth in his absence. But he had time to read with some indignation an impudent libel against his other idol, Lady Castlemaine. Some of the London brothels had recently been pulled down and the wits had been busy with the subject. One of them concocted a document entitled 'The Poor Whores' Petition to the most splendid, illustrious, serene and eminent Lady of Pleasure, the Countess of Castlemayne'. It called upon 'Barbary', as a fellow professional, to come to the assistance of the ruined harlots of the capital. Three weeks later, another wit devised and published a 'Gracious Answer of the Most Illustrious Lady of Pleasure, the Countess of Castlemayne,' and dated it 'Given at our Closset in King Street, Westminster, *die Veneris*, 24 April 1668.'

Writes the Diarist: 'It is not very witty, but devilish severe against her and the King; and I wonder how it durst be printed and spread abroad, which shews that the times are loose and come to a great disregard of the King or Court or Government. He was in a somewhat stern mood at this time, as befitted a man who had just rescued his country from a much greater public scandal. But the times certainly were loose. The same day he heard the repulsive story recounted in the eighth chapter of the Gramont memoirs to the effect that when in 1660 Lady Carnegy was found by her husband to have committed adultery with the Duke of York, her infuriated consort first took steps to infect himself with syphilis, then deliberately infected his wife and ordered her to continue the liaison with James on every possible occasion. But this topsy-turvy vengeance failed to hit the mark, for as it happened the Duke had already decided to drop Lady Carnegy. Consequently she and her husband were the only sufferers from her lord's mad act. Pepys is unaware of the full story when he comments that Carnegy's proceeding 'is the most pernicious and full piece of revenge that ever I heard of; and he at this day owns it with great glory and looks upon the Duke of York and the world with great content in the ampleness of his revenge'.

The poor lady, in her double misery of a rejected mistress and a wife poisoned by her own husband, must have told Carnegy, either in terror of him or to make him look a fool in the end, that the liaison was continuing. As syphilis may take a long time to have serious effects and would in any case be hushed up in the case of the King's brother, it is not surprising that in his mania the Earl of Southesk, as he now was, should still be boasting of an imaginary crime eight years after he thought he had committed it.

On 7th April Mr. Pepys paid a visit to Mary Knipp's dressing-room 'and there saw the several players, men and women, go by; and pretty to see how strange they are all, one to another, after the play is done. Here I saw a wonderful pretty maid of her own, that come to undress her, and one so pretty that she says she intends not to keep her, for fear of her being undone in her service by coming to the playhouse.'

He took Knipp off in a coach to the Park and had some erotic play with her, though he was rather put off, as usual, by her paint-plastered features. But, again as usual, Knipp told him a lot of the Court gossip in which he was so intensely interested. Lady Castlemaine was mad about Charles Hart, the actor, and was loading him with presents. Beck Marshall was their go-between, a peculiar office for a Presbyterian's daughter. The King was equally mad about Moll Davis, the dancer, and that was no doubt why Barbara was trying to arouse his jealousy with Hart. Once more, Mr. Pepys had to reflect sadly upon the 'looseness of the times'.

Still in this mood, he gave a sharp answer to some people at Mrs. Turner's who were chattering about the fury of Sir Robert Holmes, a distinguished naval officer and friend of Lord Sandwich, at the marriage of Holmes' ne'er-do-well son to a good-looking girl with money, but of a family considered inferior to the Holmes clan. The girl was none other than Peg Lowther, sister of Anthony Lowther, who had married Sir William Penn's daughter, also a Peg and one of Sam's willing playthings. Mr. Pepys severely told the company that he had recently arranged the marriage of his own sister 'Pall', with a dowry amounting to only half Peg Lowther's and added that, as for young Holmes, the fellow 'should have kissed her breech before he should have had her'. Sam was a big enough man now not to care whether he further enraged Sir Robert by this emphatic expression of opinion.

At last he got going with Mrs. Burroughs again, taking extreme liberties with her in a coach in the Park, and handing her on this occasion, as a Valentine's gift, no less than twelve half-crowns, a very special concession, indicating that he must have really enjoyed himself. He gave very much less, only a shilling, to Mrs. Martin shortly afterwards, though the poor woman submitted with complete abandon to his embraces at her lodgings and begged him to find a better job for her husband. But Betty Michell never seemed to be at home unless Mr. Michell was there too.

On 21st April he took Mrs. Knipp out to supper after the

theatre and on the drive home 'had the opportunity the first time in my life to be bold with Knepp . . .' to an unprintable extent. He must have forgotten the previous occasion, when the actress had been taken home ill after one of his own parties and he had visited her in bed later in the evening, going so far as to lie on the bed with her. At any rate, the lapse of memory seems to prove that hitherto he had not formed a definite liaison with her, as Mrs. Pepys sometimes suspected.

He repeated the experiment two nights later at Vauxhall, during celebrations of the anniversary of the King's coronation, but on the following day he had worse luck in two other directions, one rather important to him. While prowling about in the Soho booksellers' quarter that morning he kept an eye lifting for 'my pretty woman that I did *baiser in las tenebras*' (kiss in the dark) 'a little while *depuis*' (ago) 'and did find her *sola*' (alone) 'in the bookshop but had not *la confidence para aller a elle*'. The Diarist was liable to these sudden fits of shyness, partly constitutional, as is often the case with highly susceptible men, and partly owing to the fear of being recognised, especially now that he was so well known, and labelled as an 'idler'. 'So lost my pains,' he goes on ruefully, 'but will another time.'

After the midday meal he 'called at Michell's and there did see Betty and that was all, for either she is shy or foolish and *su mardi* (sic) hath no mind *para laiser* me see *su moher*'. He was more willing to believe that the husband, who had not been behaving too well to his wife lately, had frightened her with jealous threats, than that Betty herself, which is more likely to have been the case, had decided to be virtuous for the future. It was only after much hesitation that she had previously yielded to his importunities. Now, after the birth and distressing death of her first child by her husband, she may well have repented of her former weakness.

These disappointments seem to have rendered Mr. Pepys rather reckless. On the 30th, 'coming home in the dusk I saw and spoke to our Nell' (this was his former cook, with whom he had 'dallied' quite considerably in the previous summer before Mrs. Pepys dismissed her on 6th August) 'and had I not

been very cold I should have taken her to Tower Hill *para*
together *et toker* her'. He had imprudently left off his waistcoat
for three or four days at the end of this month of late spring, but
the weather had suddenly turned chilly. So far Nell had not
given him away to his wife and he probably felt she would
continue to be discreet, especially as she was no longer in
Elizabeth's service, but the idea that came into his head that
evening was a risky one. He would hardly have thought of it a
few weeks earlier.

At the theatre on 5th May he got near enough to the
incomparable Lady Castlemaine to sit 'close to her fine woman,
Willson, who is indeed very handsome, but they say with child
by the King'. He discussed the play a little with Mrs. Willson
and watched every movement of that paragon among women,
her mistress, noticing how she snatched a patch from the cheek
of another of her female attendants and clapped it on her own
face, 'I suppose she feeling a pimple rising there', he adds
tenderly.

Next day he was with Knipp again, whom he found at a
friend's house, after the theatre, 'on a pallet in the dark'.
But by now the cook had come to rival the actress in the
impressionable Secretary's heart. He caught sight of Nell
while walking in Crutched Friars on 6th May 'and her *je* did
desire *venir* after me and so *elle* did see me to Tower Hill to our
back entry there that comes upon the *degres entrant* into *nostra*
garden' (steps to his own garden door), where a certain
amount of intimacy took place.

Back again after Knipp on the following day, at the King's
theatre, he was too late for the play, but on making his way
round to the back premises 'I did see Beck Marshall come
dressed off of the stage and looks mighty fine and pretty and
noble, and also Nell in her boy's clothes, mighty pretty. But
Lord! Their confidence! And how many men do hover about
them as soon as they come off the stage and how confident
they are in their talk! Here I did kiss the pretty woman newly
come, called Pegg, that was Sir Charles Sidly's mistress, a
mighty pretty woman and seems, but is not, modest.'

On the 10th he had a passage with another Peg, his old friend Peg Penn, now Mrs. Lowther. It was a Sunday. He went for a walk with her, her mother and her mother-in-law in the rain at Vauxhall. 'At the Tower wharf there we did send for a pair of old shoes for Mrs. Lowther and there I did pull the others off and put them on, *elle* being *peu* shy, but do speak *con* mighty kindness to me that she would desire me *pour su mari* if it were to be done . . .' The entry tails off into obscenities. Plain Peg had never been anything but a licentious young woman, and had the advantage, from the Diarist's point of view, of being married to a loutish husband.

At Mrs. Turner's, on the 15th, there was still more evidence to be heard of the 'looseness of the times'. 'I am told also that the Countess of Shrewsbury is brought home by the Duke of Buckingham to his house, where his Duchess saying that it was not for her and the other to live together in a house, he answered: "Why, Madam, I did think so and therefore have ordered your coach to be ready to carry you to your father's." ' Sam thought this a 'devilish' remark by the Duke. But he was assured it was true and that the Duchess was now living with her father.

Next day he managed to kiss Knipp's exceptionally pretty maid at Mrs. Knipp's own house, where he was impatiently waiting for the actress and had, one supposes, to fill in the time somehow. Fortunately, Mary Knipp was not a jealous type, like Elizabeth. It would not have mattered if she had unexpectedly arrived and caught the Secretary kissing her attendant, who was probably quite used to these favours from eager gentlemen callers on her mistress.

The 'times' continued to astonish the amorous Mr. Pepys. At Vauxhall on the 18th 'I find Mrs. Horsfield one of the veriest citizen's wives in the world, so full of little silly talk and now and then a little sillily bawdy, that I believe if you had her *sola* a man might *hazer* all with her'. As for the King himself 'he is mighty hot upon the Duchess of Richmond; in so much that upon Sunday was se'n'night, at night, after he had ordered his Guards and coach to be ready to carry him to the Park, he

did on a sudden take a pair of oars . . . and all alone, or but
one with him, go to Somersett House' (where the ducal
family lived) 'and there, the garden door not being open,
himself clamber over the walls to make a visit to her, which is
a horrid shame'. By this time Sam was getting very tired of
Charles, to whom he much preferred the monarch's brother
James. The verdict of history has gone the other way. Charles
was really not such a fool as he seemed to the sober Secretary,
whereas the Duke, when he came to the throne, made an utter
ass of himself and lost it. But to Mr. Pepys James was a
revered professional chief at this time and Charles II a
mountebank who thought more of women than wisdom.

On the 21st when, for the hundredth time Samuel 'did all
that he would' with Mrs. Martin, that lady repaid his shilling
and his promises on behalf of Mr. Martin, by presenting her
lordly lover with 'a fine starling, which was the King's and
speaks finely, which I shall be glad of . . .' Two days later he
went off to Brampton to visit his wife, ignoring Mrs. Aynsworth
on his way, but delighted to see Willet again. He proceeded
to set off for Cambridge in a strictly male party, leaving Mrs.
Pepys and the maids at Brampton for a further fortnight.
The drive had been planned as a pleasant change from the
ambiguous and disturbing atmosphere of London, of which the
much scandalised Secretary had grown more than a little sick
lately. He also badly needed to rest his eyes.

This necessity perhaps accounts for the fact that the great
amorist did not take advantage of the excursion in his usual
manner, even with his wife out of the way. On the contrary, he
behaved just like an ordinary tourist. He visited his old college
of Magdalene and other haunts—reputable ones only—of his
youth. He reminisced and looked up old—male—friends. He
did see, in the coach going back to London, 'one lady alone
that is tolerably handsome but mighty well spoken whom I
took great pleasure in talking to and did get her to read aloud
in a book she was reading . . .' It turned out to be the *Meditations on Death* of Charles I before his execution, not a subject
likely to lead to 'dalliance', unfortunately. Mr. Pepys consoled

himself for this disappointment by bursting into song, probably of a 'merry' nature. The subjects of Charles II, if not those of his father, were a very mercurial lot on the whole.

Nor did the grave mood so often induced by remembrance of things past slow down the traveller when he reached London on the evening of the 26th. He at once plunged into a round of 'merry' parties and music which he regrets prevented him from sampling Mrs. Bagwell again as soon as he had hoped.

Samuel, in his new prominence in society, was now really living a gay life and meeting many theatrical people and 'gallant blades', but he was still as hard to please with their free manners as he had been when he was an obscure clerk. He was dreadfully shocked at Vauxhall on the 30th. 'There fell into the company of Harry Killigrew, a rogue newly come back out of France, but still in disgrace at our Court, and young Newport and others, as very rogues as any in the town, who were ready to take hold of every woman that come by them. And so to supper in an arbour: but, Lord! their mad bawdy talk did make my heart ake! And here I first understood by their talk the meaning of the company that lately were called Ballers; Harris telling how it was by a meeting of some young blades, where he was among them, and my Lady Bennet and her ladies' (both name and title are given ironically to the well-known procuress already mentioned) 'and their there dancing naked and all the roguish things in the world. But, Lord! what loose cursed company was this, that I was in tonight, though full of wit; and worth a man's being in for once, to know the nature of it and their manner of talk and lives.'

As in the case of his comment on the pornographic *L'Escole des Filles*, it is the very voice of a sober, modest citizen, though Sam was now one of the most prominent administrators in the country and could give a point or two even to 'blades' in the number and variety of his conquests among the other sex. This ambivalence makes the Diarist almost a case for the psychiatrist's notebook. Hard worker, devoted husband, regular churchgoer and serious musician, he was yet capable of seducing young married women who came to see him on business, keeping a definitely disreputable mistress and 'towzling' his maids whenever he got the chance. It was unusual, even in the seventeenth century; for Samuel was no hypocrite, except in so far as all of us are obliged to be, as the mere fact of the frankness of his journal shows. Not one of the many pompous frauds of the nineteenth century, for instance, would have dared to record their sexual misdemeanours even in cipher, let alone with such utter objectivity as the Secretary did.

Not content with such well tried members of Mrs. Martin's circle as her sister and Mrs. Burroughs, Mr. Pepys now added her 'jolly' landlady, Mrs. Craggs, to his list. After the usual phrase indicating intercourse with Betty Martin, he calmly adds, on 1st June, 'did once *toker la* thigh *de su* landlady'. Moreover, Mrs. Bagwell now again comes into the picture, after an absence of several months, though he had tried unsuccessfully to renew his acquaintance with her more than once lately. 'I to my little mercer's Finch, that lives now in the Minores, where I have left my cloak, and did here *baiser su moher* a *belle femme* and . . . down to Deptford where I have not been many a day and there it being dark I did by agreement *aller a la* house *de* Bagwell and there after a little playing and *baisando* we did go up in the dark *a su camera*' (her bedroom), where the liaison was revived in a scene too precisely delineated for quotation.

On 5th June he decided on yet another excursion, for his eyes were still troubling him so seriously that he could hardly read. He rode to Brampton with Will Hewer, collected his wife and the maids and went by coach to Oxford, Bath and the west country, from which both Elizabeth and Deb had originally come. They took the waters at Bath and met some of Deb's relatives and friends, who made a favourable impression on both husband and wife.

Samuel, out of his keen interest in the girl, was particularly touched by the welcome given her in Marsh Street, Bath, where she had been born. 'But, Lord!' he writes, 'the joy that was among the old poor people of the place to see Mrs. Willet's daughter, it seems her mother being a brave woman and mightily beloved. And so' (Deb's uncle) 'brought us a back way by surprize to his house, where a substantial good house and well furnished; and did give us good entertainment' (including strawberries, wine and rum punch) 'where comes in another poor woman, who hearing that Deb was here did come running hither and with her eyes so full of tears and heart so full of joy that she could not speak when she come in, that it made me weep too: I protest that I was not able to speak to her, which I would have done, to have diverted her tears. His wife' (i.e. Deb's aunt) 'a good woman and so sober and substantial as I was never more pleased anywhere. Servant-maid 2s.'

This charming passage shows the sometimes rakish Mr. Pepys in quite a sentimental mood. No one would dream that he was all the time firmly determined to seduce the central figure of all this tearful rejoicing. It is certain that the devotion of these humble and defenceless people to the prospective victim, much moved though he was by it at the time, did not for a single second give him pause in his design, though he must have realised that sooner or later his plans would be bound to lead to tears of vexation, to say the least of it, rather than joy, for Deb and her circle.

The masculine seventeenth century mind, when alight with lust, simply did not work that way; but at any rate Sam did not kiss anybody on that pathetic occasion, merely tipping the maid's outstretched hand instead of her chin.

Despite this admirable restraint, Mrs. Pepys appeared perversely out of humour, no doubt owing to Deb's presence, for most of the time occupied by this highly enjoyable trip. Samuel guessed that she was brooding over Mrs. Pierce again, for he had jocularly but tactlessly referred to the lady in question once or twice.

They returned to London on the 17th. On the 18th 'at noon home to dinner, where my wife still in a melancholy, fusty humour and crying and do not tell me plainly what it is; but I by little words find that she hath heard of my going to plays and carrying people abroad every day in her absence . . .' He took her for a drive that afternoon and suggested attending a new play, but she sulkily declined this treat. About one o'clock that night she 'goes out of the bed to the girl's bed, which did trouble me, she crying and sobbing without telling the cause. By and by she comes back to me and still crying . . .' Elizabeth was certainly behaving like a child half her age.

There was an alarm of fire an hour later, and everyone got up. Samuel went out and watched the flames of a house in Mincing Lane burn the building to ashes. After a while he returned and slept a little, then 'about nine rose' to find his wife still 'blubbering'. At last it all came out. She wanted to leave a husband who no longer loved her and go to live in France. She did not want to stand in the way of his debaucheries. She had had enough of his neglect.

Mr. Pepys was not so concerned as he might have been in the earlier years of their marriage. He kept calm, denied her accusations and promised to take her to France next year. He also promised himself to take her about a bit more and did so, carefully avoiding Mary Knipp and Mrs. Pierce while he was in Elizabeth's company. Peace eventually seemed to have been restored, but he could not help feeling that the domestic atmosphere remained charged with not altogether vague menace. Nevertheless, Mrs. Daniel, Betty Michell—who remained cool—and of course Betty Martin received the usual attentions, in the first and third cases intimate.

That month he was obliged to consult an oculist, who prescribed drops and bleeding. Early in July Betty Michell gave birth to another child, a girl. No doubt her pregnancy had had something to do with her recent coldness to Mr. Pepys. Mrs. Pepys assisted the midwife at the birth and both Pepyses went to see the mother afterwards, Elizabeth consenting to stand godmother to the baby.

More unpleasant stories about the King and more pleasant experiences with Mrs. Daniel followed, as well as a further temporary row between Mrs. Pepys and Deb about a mislaid hood, which 'vexed' Sam much more than it need have done.

But any acrimonious exchanges between his wife and the girl he was still determined to seduce put his nerves on edge.

On 24th July he arranged with the Duke of York to double-cross Buckingham by a letter, ostensibly from James but really written by Samuel, calling for an account of duties and procedures at the Navy Office. The object was to have a clear statement to make to Buckingham when, as seemed probable, that mercurial gentleman took it into his head to raise still further his already high political status by the well tried method of wiping the floor with a Government Department.

Sam was now nearly blind, the oculist's treatment having proved worse than useless, driving him to the expedient of 'paper tubes'. But he still followed pretty women about the streets, criticised stage-plays, paintings and engravings, read books and composed music, as well as sticking as closely as ever to his office work.

Sometimes, however, he would get his wife or one of the more literate servants to read to him in the evenings. After supper on 10th August 'my wife to read a ridiculous book I bought to-day of the History of the Taylors' Company and all the while Deb did comb my head and I did *toker* her with my *main para* very great pleasure . . .' It is possible that he had purchased this dull book on purpose not to have his attention distracted from Deb while it was being read to him. But here again he was running a certain risk, with his wife actually in the same room and perhaps as bored with the book as he was, despite her dutiful compliance with his wishes. Yet undoubtedly the experienced and prudent amorist took care to pursue his erotic explorations in such a way that even if Elizabeth happened to glance up she would not notice them.

Both Mr. and Mrs. Pepys had an experience on 19th August which might have warned them against giving too free a rein to the green-eyed monster. Apparently, however, it did not and Samuel appears to have regarded the affair as merely a nuisance. 'In the evening, being busy above, a great cry I hear and go down and what should it be but Jane' (Jane Birch, a normally quiet, sleepy girl of considerable physical strength who, for a wonder, had never particularly attracted her master, probably for the very reason that she was so big and strong) 'in a fit of direct raving which lasted half an hour. Beyond four or five of our strength to keep her down . . .'

Jane was in love with Tom Edwards, another of the servants, and had reason to suspect that he was trying to shuffle out of the marriage which had been arranged between them. 'So that I must rid my hands of them, which troubles me and the more because my head is now busy upon other greater things . . .' He meant his public prospects, which were now once more endangered.

For on the 30th Lord Brouncker told him that 'the Duke of Buckingham did within few hours say that he had enough to turn us all out: which I am not sorry for at all, for I know the world will judge me to go for company' (i.e. leaving because his colleagues would be leaving) 'and my eyes are such as I am not able to do the business of my Office as I used and would desire to do while I am in it'. He was weary again and longing for retirement. But he was to serve his country for many long years yet.

On 1st September, at Bartholomew Fair, after a disappointing visit to Betty Michell, 'saw several sights; among others the mare that tells money and many things to admiration; and among others come to me, when she was bid to go to him of the company that most loved a pretty wench in a corner. And this did cost me 12d. to the horse, which I had flung him before, and did give me occasion to *baiser* a mighty *belle fille* that was in the house, that was exceeding plain' (i.e. a rough, simple creature) 'but *fort belle*. At night going home I went to my—' female—'bookseller's in Duck Lane and find her weeping in the shop, so as *ego* could not have any discourse *con* her nor ask the reason, so departed and took coach home and taking coach was set on by a wench that was naught' (i.e. ugly) 'and would have gone along with me to her lodging in Shoe Lane, but *ego* did *donner* her a shilling . . . and left her.'

This somewhat incoherent and slightly acid narrative reflects the nervous and worried condition of the Diarist at this period.

Half-blind, frustrated of his designs on Betty Michell and Deb Willet, knowing that there was a conspiracy to deprive him of his official post, but as resolute, both for pleasure and for business, as ever, Samuel seemed to be on the down-grade, though he would not admit it.

It is significant of his irritable mood that he declined to lend Mrs. Daniel any money at this time, 'having not opportunity *para hazer allo* thing *mit* her'. The sudden break, for the first time, into German—though the *mit* is probably a mis-spelling of the Dutch *met*, more familiar to Englishmen at that period— adds yet another foreign language to the deliberate obscurities of the cipher.

All the same, on the 16th 'dressing myself I did begin *para toker* the breasts of my maid Jane' (the previously neglected perpetrator of the recent violent scene of jealousy over Tom Edwards was now belatedly joining the Secretary's list) 'which *elle* did give way to more than usual heretofore' (perhaps on account of Tom's defection) 'so I have a design to try more when I can bring it to'.

Nor could he, even now, keep away from Knipp, in spite of her rouge. He dined with her on the 17th, drove her to the theatre and presented her with five guineas. On the 26th, in West-minster Hall, he made frantic signs, at a distance, to Doll Lane, but for some reason or other she ignored his gestures of invitation to the Swan. He had to be content with the company of a Guards officer at dinner.

A gap of thirteen days now occurs in the Diary. Pepys was off on another holiday in the country, Suffolk way. He did not return until 11th October, when he had his household once more about him, including Deb, who combed his hair on the 13th, rousing him to a pitch of amorous excitement which he could scarcely control.

Lord Sandwich had returned from Spain on the 27th of the previous month, loaded with debt, but maintaining as great state as ever. His attentive cousin decided to give his too careless patron some tactful advice, but first he felt that he simply must have a private coach of his own. He had often been ashamed lately of appearing in a hackney among his grand friends, especially in the Park. He bid £50 for a vehicle 'which pleased me mightily', and after some bargaining got it for £53. Elizabeth was 'out of herself for joy almost' when he showed it to her.

He still could not get near Sandwich, but his resolution to do so was confirmed by a story he heard from Pierce on the 23rd. It seemed that Sir Charles Sedley and Lord Buckhurst, who shared Nell Gwyn's favours at that time, had been 'running up and down all the night with their arses bare through the streets; and at last fighting and being beat by the watch and clapped up all night; and my Lord Chief Justice Keeling hath laid the constable by the heels to answer it next sessions; which is a horrid shame'. He uses the same expression as he had used about Charles' balcony-climbing at Somerset House to get at the Duchess of Richmond, and means by it an honest patriot's disgust at the disorderly behaviour of the rulers and aristocrats of the country, only too easy to imitate by those ambitious of similar positions of authority.

He goes on to record the Duke of Buckingham's political pre-eminence, his hostility to Sir William Coventry and the Duke of York, Lady Castlemaine's break with him, and the King's coarse revels with Sedley and Buckhurst, to the rage of Charles' brother. When James reprimanded one of the circle the fellow merely boasted of the royal confidence, and cynically begged the Duke's pardon for having it. No wonder Sam felt that the nation had fallen on evil days. But his personal optimism gave him no inkling of the private misfortune that was almost instantly to burst upon him.

II

The Sky Falls

IT was on Sunday, 25th October 1668, after supper, that
Mr. Pepys' world crashed about his ears. The catastrophe
was one which might have been foreseen, but he records
it as if he could never have dreamed of such a thing. 'After
supper, to have my head combed by Deb, which occasioned the
greatest sorrow to me that ever I knew in this world, for my
wife, coming up suddenly, did find me embracing the girl . . .
I was at a wonderful loss upon it and the girle also and I
endeavoured to put it off but my wife was struck mute and
grew angry and so her voice come to her grew quite out of
order and I to say little, but to bed, and my wife said little also,
but could not sleep all night, but about two in the morning
waked me and cried, and fell to tell me as a great secret that
she was a Roman Catholique and had received the Holy
Sacrament, which troubled me, but I took no notice of it, but
she went on from one thing to another till at last it appeared
plainly her trouble was at what she saw, but yet I did not know
how much she saw, and therefore said nothing to her. But after
her much crying and reproaching me with inconstancy and
preferring a sorry girl before her, I did give her no provocation
but did promise all fair usage to her and love and foreswore
any hurt that I did with her, till at last she seemed to be at
ease again . . .'

The damage was done, however. The expert had been caught
out at last, after all these years, by one of the most jealous
women he knew, his own wife. The circumstances were most
unfortunate, for Deb was no empty-headed slut, but a well-
connected and well-educated girl, whose relatives both husband

and wife liked very much. And now Mrs. Pepys had sworn, naturally enough, to dismiss her.

On his return from the office next day for the midday meal the Diarist found a grim atmosphere. Both women looked very glum, and Elizabeth would not speak to the maid. He made himself scarce for the rest of the day. 'Anon to bed, where about midnight she wakes me and there falls foul of me again, affirming that she saw me hug and kiss the girl; the latter I denied and truly, the other I confessed and no more, and upon her pressing me did offer to give her under my hand that I would never see Mrs. Pierce more nor Knepp, but did promise her particular demonstrations of my true love to her, owning some indiscretions in what I did, but that there was no harm in it. She at last upon these promises was quiet . . .'

It was all he could do; but the next night Elizabeth kept him awake almost till daybreak with her wrathful complaints and threats of telling everyone they knew of his disgraceful conduct. She even got out of bed and lit a candle to curse him by. He calmed her at last, writing a note to Deb next day with a brief report of the position, asking her to burn this communication, which the honest young woman duly did. The next few days passed off fairly quietly, but with great anxiety on the Diarist's part, for he still did not know quite what his wife meant to do.

On 1st November he writes: 'I cannot be informed how poor Deb stands with her mistress, but I fear she will put her away and the truth is, though it be much against my mind, and to my trouble, yet I think that it will be fit that she should be gone, for my wife's peace and mine, for she cannot but be offended at the sight of her, my wife having conceived this jealousy of me with reason, and therefore for that and other reasons of expense, it will be best for me to let her go, but I shall love and pity her.'

A day or two later he found that Mrs. Pepys had already discussed the matter with the girl's aunt who had been very reasonable about it and agreed to Deb's going. On the 4th she went out to look for another situation, returning the next morning, apparently unsuccessful in the search. Mrs. Pepys kept the girl out of her husband's sight. She was no longer allowed to dress him, let alone comb his hair. He was so distracted at this period that he entered some items of his journal under the wrong date, though he afterwards corrected the mistake. His genuine distress and sympathy for both the injured parties comes out again and again in lengthy passages of the Diary. Elizabeth gave him no peace, even in the maid's now rare presence. Yet the girl still stayed on in these uncomfortable conditions.

On the 9th, in desperation, 'I did by a little note which I flung to Deb, advise her that I did continue to deny that ever I kissed her, and so she might govern herself. The truth is that I did adventure upon God's pardoning me this lie, knowing how heavy a thing it would be for me to the ruin of the poor girle, and next knowing that if my wife should know all it were impossible ever for her to be at peace with me again and so our whole lives would be uncomfortable. The girl read and as I bid her returned me the note, flinging it to me in passing by.' She had to deny the kissing, which if admitted would apparently seal both her fate and Sam's. So they *had* kissed, and not either casually or by way of greeting or leave-taking, but as lovers. The distinction between the meeting of lips in this fashion and mere fondling was perhaps more real in the seventeenth century than it is today, when they generally go together. In any case it is clear that Mrs. Pepys would have pardoned a playful slap and tickle, but not a 'hugging' kiss. The Diarist had evidently roused the girl at last, and had been interrupted on the very verge of seducing her. Hence, in part, the mournful tone of these entries, though of course they were mainly motivated by his perfectly genuine love for his wife.

On the 10th Elizabeth told her husband that the maid had 'confessed', giving him a dreadful fright. He continued stoutly to deny that he had ever kissed Deb in any passionate way. His wife then informed him that, by way of contrast with his own behaviour, she herself had virtuously refused most advantageous offers from Lords Sandwich, Pepys' own cousin

and patron, and Hinchingbrooke, Sandwich's heir. She made
such a tremendous scene that Sam eventually promised that he
would himself order Deb out of the house.

He actually took this step on the 12th, in his wife's presence,
'with tears in my eyes', in which the poor girl joined, but
hoping she would be intelligent enough to realise that he was
not really angry with her. On the 13th 'Deb has been abroad
to-day and is come home and says she has got a place to go to,
so as she will be gone to-morrow morning. This troubled me
and the truth is I have a good mind to have the maidenhead
of this girl, which I should not doubt to have if *je* could get
time *para* be *con* her. But she will be gone and I not know
whither.' Some ardours would have been damped by all that
had happened since the intervention of Mrs. Pepys. But it
is highly characteristic of Samuel that he could not bear to
think of the cup being dashed from his lips at the very last
moment, even now. He determined to slake it, come what
might.

A curious detail of this affair follows, recorded without
further comment by the Diarist on the 14th, when Deb had
gone and all was quiet again (for the moment). 'I must here
remember that I have lain with my *moher* as a husband more
times since this falling out than in I believe twelve months
before. And with more pleasure to her than I think in all the
time of our marriage before.' During the past fortnight passionate quarrels had been ended temporarily by reconciliations
equally passionate, on the husband's side largely as a matter of
policy, on the wife's owing to the stimulation of one emotion
by another.

Somehow or other, from incautious remarks by Elizabeth,
he got the impression that the girl had gone to Holborn, to
an employer named Allbon. He made enquiries locally and 'I
find that this Dr. Allbon is a kind of poor broken fellow that
dare not shew his head nor be known where he is gone'.
He tracked Dr. Allbon as far as Fleet Street. On the 18th
'I did go by coach directly to Somerset House and there
enquired among the porters there for Dr. Allbon and the first

I spoke with told me he knew him and that he was newly gone into Lincoln's Inn Fields, but whither he could not tell me . . .'

Mr. Pepys returned to the charge that evening. At last he found a porter who agreed to deliver a message to the doctor. Sam gave the man the girl's name 'and sent him to see how she did from her friend in London and no other token. He goes while I walk in Somerset House, walk there in the Court; at last he comes back and tells me she is well and that I may see her if I will, but no more. So I could not be commanded by my reason but I must go this very night and so by coach, it being now dark, I to her, close by my tailor's, and she come into the coach to me and *je* did *baiser* her . . .'

He was jubilant, but also anxious and prudent. Controlling himself with difficulty, he told her 'to have a care of her honour and to fear God and suffer no man *para avoir* to do *con* her as *je* have done, which she promised'. He was very much afraid, and with good reason, that she might take to evil courses under her new employers. He wanted, for once, to keep this pretty little virgin all to himself. It is evident that this infatuation was the most serious he had experienced since his marriage. He gave her some money—twenty shillings—and told her to keep in touch with him through his bookseller. She seemed to agree to everything, and promised to write.

But next day, at noon, he was thunderstruck to hear his wife 'call me all the false, rotten-hearted rogues in the world, letting me understand that I was with Deb yesterday, which, thinking it impossible for her ever to understand, I did a while deny, but at last did, for the ease of my mind and hers, and for ever to discharge my heart of this wicked business I did confess all'. Elizabeth swore 'she would slit the nose of this girle and be gone herself this very night from me and did there demand 3 or £400 from me to buy my peace, that she might be gone without making any noise, or else protested that she would make all the world know of it'.

Samuel 'with most perfect confusion of face and heart, and sorrow and shame, in the greatest agony in the world' confided in his chief clerk, William Hewer, with whom at first he had not got on very well, though Mrs. Pepys had always liked him, possibly just because her husband didn't. For the last year or two, however, the irascible Secretary had thought more highly of him. Hewer persuaded Elizabeth to make up the quarrel on condition that Samuel signed a paper undertaking never to see or speak to Deb again. The Diarist agreed to this arrangement (though most reluctantly and very doubtful whether he would be able to keep to it) with the result that the reconciliation was sealed by passionate conjugal embraces that night.

On the 20th Pepys sent Hewer to Deb 'to tell her that I had told my wife all of my being with her the other night, that so if my wife should send she might not make the business worse by denying it'. But to the errant husband's horror, on returning home, 'I find my wife upon her bed in a horrible rage afresh, calling me all the bitter names, and rising did fall to revile me in the bitterest manner in the world and could not refrain to strike me and pull my hair'. There was more talk of slitting Deb's nose. Then Hewer, hearing the uproar, entered the room. While he tried to pacify Mrs. Pepys, Samuel flung himself, 'in a sad, desperate condition' upon a bed in another room.

Eventually Hewer told him that 'if I would call Deb whore under my hand and write to her that I hated her and would never see her more' all would be well. Sam boggled, as well he might, at the word 'whore'. He wrote the required note omitting this offensive term. But Elizabeth tore the letter to shreds. 'Whore' had to go in, or else, etc. The clerk, with his back to the raging wife, gave his master a solemn wink, which the latter immediately understood. Sam then wrote a sentence to the effect that Deb's behaviour with him had made him suspect that she might be a whore and that he therefore did not wish to see her again. This amendment satisfied Mrs. Pepys. She gave the note to Hewer to take to the girl, and smiled benevolently upon her husband.

Next day, in the office, Hewer returned the letter to Pepys, telling him he had not shown it to Deb, but merely informed her, as charitably as he could, that his master did not want to see her again. In the evening peace reigned once more at the conjugal board and bed. Mrs. Pepys had scored a decisive and lasting victory over her sinful spouse. He had been terribly frightened by this affair, as well as humiliated and chastened for the time being. He did see Deb again, more than once, but only in the street. On a single occasion he did actually take her to a tavern, where, however, she refused intercourse. He never forgot her. On the very last page of the Diary he refers to her with regret. It is certain that he suffered nearly as much from the frustration of his passion for her as he did from the awful threat of his wife to leave him on her account. For once in this disorderly world a philanderer—to call Sam nothing worse— had been fearfully punished for his defiance of sexual convention, for on top of everything else he even had the mortification of realising, as a man of the world, that he would almost certainly be responsible for the corruption by others of a virgin of whom he had been so deeply, so almost paternally, fond.

It was not until 7th December that 'this afternoon, passing through Queen's Street, I saw pass by our coach on foot Deb, which, God forgive me, did put me into some new thoughts of her, and for her, but durst not shew them, and I think my wife did not see her, but I did get my thoughts free of her as soon as I could'. In fact, he hardly dared to look at any woman now and was living if not like an anchorite, at any rate like the steadiest of faithful husbands. Mrs. Pepys kept him up to the mark by watching him openly in mixed company and even after he was asleep, telling him he sometimes seemed to be thinking of Deb in his dreams.

On the 18th she reported indirect news of her rival. 'She hath heard of Deb's being mighty fine and gives out that she hath a friend that gives her money and this my wife believes to be me . . . but I did pacify all . . . and I hope it will be our last struggle from this business . . .' He was fairly well resigned by this time; but he must have felt a twinge of remorse, being the man he was, at Deb's new 'finery'. It could only mean that she was living an immoral life, into which he himself, her sincere lover, had thrust her.

There was more trouble with Elizabeth on the night of

12th January 1669. She accused Samuel of having been 'seen
in a hackney coach—' the Pepyses of course now had a private
coach of their own—'with the glasses up with Deb, but could
not tell the time nor was sure I was he. I did, as I might truly,
deny it and was mightily troubled, but all would not serve.
At last, about one o'clock, she come to my side of the bed and
drew my curtaine open and with the tongs red hot at the ends,
made as if she did design to pinch me with them, at which in
dismay I rose up and with a few words she laid them down, and
did little by little, very sillily, let all the discourse fall'. Samuel's
patience under these conditions is something to wonder at in
the seventeenth century, when most husbands would have
given their wives a terrific thrashing for a mere threat of
scratching, let alone branding with fire-irons. His phenomenal
mildness on this occasion gives the measure of his repentance.
But it is clear that Mrs. Pepys had forgotten Deb as little as he
had.

Elizabeth also made one or two scenes, quite without
justification, about Mrs. Knipp, Mrs. Pierce and even Jane
Birch, their cook-maid. It is true that in the past, before and
since Deb's time, Pepys had had some passages with all three
of these women, but he had not been near any of them since
the catastrophe. Nevertheless, Mrs. Pepys 'did believe me false
to her with Jane and did rip up three or four silly circumstances
of her not rising till I come out of my chamber and her letting
me thereby see her dressing herself; and that I must needs go
into her chamber and was naught' (naughty) 'with her . . .'
It was all rubbish. In due course he convinced her of the fact,
but not before she had made arrangements, afterwards cancelled,
to sleep with Jane herself in future.

All the same, Jane had to go, and on 8th February was duly
dismissed with her affianced, Tom Edwards.

Mr. Pepys' unwonted continence was now drawing to an
end. He was finding it impossible to make so drastic a break
with the habits of a lifetime. On the 17th, in Whitehall, while
hurrying from one business appointment to another 'I had a
pleasant rencontre of a lady in mourning that by the little light

I had seemed handsome. I passing by her I did observe she looked back again and again upon me, I suffering her to go before and it being now duske . . .' He followed her about for some considerable time, at last spoke to her, but, seeing his boy waiting for him a little way off '*je* durst not go out *con* her, which vexed me, and my mind, God forgive me, did run *apres* her *toute* that night . . .'

This was an ominous sign, but worse was to come. The next lips that Pepys kissed were, positively, those of a corpse. On the 23rd, at Westminster Abbey, 'we did see, by particular favour, the body of Queen Katherine of Valois; and I had the upper part of her body in my hands and I did kiss her mouth, reflecting upon it that I did kiss a Queen and that this was my birthday, thirty-six years old, that I did first kiss a Queen'. This macabre experience is not stated to have aroused Elizabeth's jealousy, the Queen having been buried in 1457. But the passage is not only highly characteristic of the Diarist's peculiar psychology but also suggests that he had by no means turned over a new leaf, for all his protestations and abject obedience to his wife. The gesture would hardly have occurred to anyone but an incorrigible amorist. Perhaps it was as well that he had a shockingly bad cold this month and could hardly speak. His eyes, too, were getting worse and worse.

During the next few days he had to ask God to forgive him several times for 'looking on pretty women', Elizabeth's censorship of these aberrations having apparently relaxed a little. On 4th March he could stand it no longer, and 'slunk out to Bagwell's and there saw her and her mother and our late maid Nell, who cried for joy to see me. but I had no time for pleasure then . . . having a month's mind' (i.e. a very great mind) '*para* have had a bout with Nell, which I believe I could have had and may another time'. Mrs. Pepys nagged him for his long absence, but on the wrong tack, guessing that he had gone to see Pierce or Knipp. He reassured her as well as he could, and, as usual, succeeded in the end.

On the 11th she started teasing him, obviously with a grim intention underneath the banter, with a story about a new and very handsome chambermaid she had hired. He believed the tale, secretly delighted, but primly told her that the girl would be in no danger from him, though he would be glad to 'look upon' her.

Next day matters took a more serious turn. He found his wife 'alone in the dark, in a hot fit of railing against me, upon some news she has this day heard of Deb's living very fine and with black spots' (the fashionable patches for the cheeks) 'and speaking ill words of her mistress . . .' It was Elizabeth, apparently, that Deb was alleged to have been abusing, not without some excuse. Pepys swore, quite correctly, that he had no idea where Deb was or what she was doing, adding in the Diary, significantly enough 'though God knows that my devil that is within me do wish that I could'.

Unfortunately Mrs. Pepys also added something, viz. that the news had caused her to cancel the arrangements for the handsome maid and hire another who was pock-marked. Sam said never a word in reply to this information, though he must have ground his teeth a little. But there was no relying on anything his wife said nowadays, all her announcements having some relation to her jealousy of him.

On the 17th, at a casual visit to the Michells, he heard that Doll Lane 'is suddenly brought to bed at her sister's lodging and gives it out that she is married but there is no such thing certainly, she never mentioning it before, but I have cause to rejoice that I have not seen her a great while . . .' So at any rate she could not, like her sister on a similar occasion, accuse Sam of being the father of the expected child.

On the 18th the originally hired handsome maid did in fact turn up to enter upon her duties, much to Samuel's amazement and delight. For the moment, however, he had something else to do. On the 24th he set out for Maidstone in his own coach, with two male friends. On the way he called to see a certain Captain Allen, a former colleague, for reasons not unconnected with the reawakened erotic susceptibilities of the Diarist. Captain Allen had a daughter, Rebecca, whom Pepys had kissed 'very often' in April 1661. She had married a Lieutenant

Jowles a year or so later, but in 1667 Jowles had been imprisoned for challenging his Captain to a duel, and Sam had hardly seen Rebecca since.

Captain Allen was not at home; but the caller had a glimpse of Rebecca through the window, and liked what he saw. On the way home he called again and, while the others played cards, talked over old times with Rebecca. 'And there I had the liberty to salute her often and pull off her glove' (Sam took an interest in girls' hands which approached fetishism) 'where her hand mighty moist and she mighty free in kindness to me and *je* do not at all doubt that I might have had that that I would have desired *de elle* had I had time to have carried her to Cobham, as she, upon my proposing it, was very willing to go, for *elle* is a whore, that is certain, but a very brave and comely one . . . did get her to the street door and there to her *su* breasts and *baiser* her without any force and *credo* that I might have had all else, but it was not time nor place.'

It is clear that Samuel was practically his old pre-Deb self again. The tone of this entry is identical with that of the great majority of erotic passages in the Diary. It is true that he was staying at Chatham just then, having left his wife for a few days in London. He rejoined her, without incident, on the 28th.

It seems almost superfluous to add that he was nosing round after Mrs. Bagwell on the 29th, and also taking a good look at the new chambermaid, whose name was Matt, 'a proper and very comely maid . . .' At the New Exchange, on 7th April, he renewed acquaintance with an old friend, a seamstress named Betty Smith. And to crown all, two days later he was with Mrs. Martin, 'the first time I have been with her since her husband went last to sea, which is I think a year since . . . But, Lord! to hear how sillily she tells the story of her sister Doll's being a widow and lately brought to bed and her husband . . . drowned, that was at sea with her husband but by chance dead at sea, cast away. When God knows she hath played the whore and is sillily forced at this time, after she was brought to bed, to forge this story.'

Mr. Pepys did not care much for Doll, though he was glad enough of her company if Betty was not to be had.

On the 13th, at Whitehall, 'being in the courtyard, as God would have it, I spied Deb, which made my heart and head to work . . .' He immediately dismissed Hewer, who was with him, and set off in pursuit of the girl. She was with two commonplace-looking women and a man, and was shabbily dressed. The party descended into the Palace underground chapel. Pepys followed and spoke to his adored one, 'and did get her *pour dire* me *ou* she *demeurs* now and did charge her say nothing of me that I had *vu elle*, which she did promise'. So now he had her address. But he was in a terrible state all the rest of that day in case he should give the game away, by some peculiarity of manner or undue agitation, when he came to tell his wife how he had spent his time. He was also not sure whether Hewer had seen the girl or not. 'My great pain,' he characteristically adds, 'is lest God Almighty should suffer me to find out this girl, whom indeed I love and with a bad amour, but I will pray to God to give me grace to forbear it.' In other words he was desperately keen to revive the affair, and as desperately terrified that Elizabeth might suspect the plan.

On the 15th he took a hackney to Aldgate Street, to the address Deb had given him, and sent the coachman to enquire whether Mrs. Hunt, the girl's aunt, was at home. The man came back to say she was not and Pepys, in a sudden fit of anxiety, drove away, not daring to make any further enquiries. He was in a helpless state of indecision about the whole business.

Later in the day, after an inconclusive talk with Mrs. Bagwell, he saw Deb from his coach, going up Holborn Hill, while he was driving down it. 'I saw her and she me, but she made no stop, but seemed unwilling to speak to me; so I away on, but then stopped and 'light and after her and overtook her at the end of Hosier Lane in Smithfield and without standing in the street desired her to follow me and I led her into a little blind alehouse within the walls and there she and I alone fell to talk and *baiser la* and *toker su mammailles*, but she mighty coy and I hope modest . . .' He gave her another twenty shillings and more good advice, pleased to find her, contrary to Elizabeth's reports, still in her former humble condition. Deb agreed to meet him in Westminster Hall on the following Monday—a rather surprising choice of place, where he was bound to be seen by acquaintances, but by now he had almost swung to the opposite extreme from timidity, so elated did he feel at the prospect of a renewal of the intrigue.

However, Deb did not keep the appointment at Westminster. Sam did not know whether to be glad of her 'modesty' and his escape from further temptation, or exasperated at yet another check to his designs. Sad to say, he consoled himself with the 'whore' Doll Lane, Mrs. Martin having gone to see her husband at Portsmouth.

Mrs. Pepys showed no signs of jealousy at this time. In fact, it was Samuel's turn to be jealous, for it seemed that for some time she had been greatly taken with a Mr. Sheres, a poet, and 'a very civil and worthy man, I think; but only it do seem to imply some little neglect of me'. Mr. Sheres gave her some drawing lessons.

On the 26th Samuel and his wife were at the Temple Gate, in their coach, after dropping Sheres at Temple Bar, when 'I spied Deb with another gentlewoman and Deb winked on me and smiled, but undiscovered' (i.e. by Mrs. Pepys) 'and I was glad to see her'. Stimulated by this incident, and also relieved by the departure of Sheres for Tangier on 1st May, Mr. Pepys, on the 4th, drove to the girl's address and sent the coachman to enquire for her. He returned with the information that Deb had left for Greenwich 'to one Marys's, a tanner' (presumably in connection with employment there) 'at which I was glad, hoping to have opportunity to find her out', since he often visited Greenwich on official business. It is typical of this strange affair that he was rather pleased than otherwise at not having found the girl at home. If he had, 'it is forty to one but I had been abroad, God forgive me—' i.e. out for the rest of the day, with the practical certainty of a terrible row with Elizabeth in the evening.

He made 'private vows' that night not to go to Greenwich for the present, much though he desired to do so. On the 7th there was an unpleasant reminder that Mrs. Pepys was still wide awake in this connection. Driving through Bow with her, he noticed 'some young gentlewomen at a door' and so, unfortunately, did his wife. She cried out that he 'knew well enough it was that damned place where Deb dwelt—' and Sam lost his temper, for it was nothing of the kind. He ordered the coach to turn and pass the door again, by this manoeuvre convincing Elizabeth that she was mistaken. It was a disagreeable episode, however, and confirmed Samuel in his resolve not to pursue Deb to Greenwich. He had come to the conclusion that whatever he did in relation to that girl his wife would be sure to find it out sooner or later, with results that would not bear thinking about. And in fact there is no evidence that he ever saw Deb again after the 'winking' meeting at Temple Gate on 26th April.

Betty Michell, too, the other more or less respectable object of Pepys' extra-marital affections, was receding into the background of his interests. On the 9th he caught sight of her in the distance near St. Margaret's, Westminster, 'but she is become much a plainer woman than she was a girl'.

The perennial Mrs. Martin, however, had not lost her fascination for him and on the 10th he looked her up. But she was still at Portsmouth. He saw Doll and Mrs. Cragg, and also kissed a new maid at the Swan. But it seemed as though the great amorist was beginning to lose his grip as he approached his forties and the trouble with his eyes increased steadily.

At last, on the 12th, he renewed definite relations with Betty Martin, though apparently without much relish. 'Lord!' he exclaims. 'How silly the woman talks of her great entertainment' (at Portsmouth) 'and how all the gentry come to visit her and that she believes her husband is worth 6 or £700, which nevertheless I am glad of, but I doubt they will spend it as fast.' The tone is wearily condescending. Entries in the Diary this month show little sign of 'mirth' anywhere. On the 16th Mr. Pepys drafted an application to the Duke of York, head of the Navy, 'for leave to spend three or four months out of the Office' to rest his eyes.

The Duke consented to this petition on the 19th. Pepys was to go to Holland, but to give out that he was merely leaving London for a while. He took leave of the King, who was most sympathetic, and of Betty Michell in her husband's absence. 'And here *je* did *baiser elle*,' he adds with a touch of his old swagger, 'but had not opportunity *para hazer* some with her, as I would have offered if *je* had had it.'

On 31st May 1669 he pens the last entry of the Diary. 'And thus ends all that I doubt I shall ever be able to do with my own eyes in the keeping of my Journal, I being not able to do it any longer, having done now so long as to undo my eyes almost every time that I take a pen in my hand; and therefore, whatever comes of it, I must forbear: and therefore resolve from this time forward to have it kept by my people' (his servants and clerks) 'in longhand and must therefore be contented to set down no more than is fit for them and all the world to know; or if there be any thing, which cannot be much, now my amours to Deb are past, and my eyes hindering me in almost all other pleasures, I must endeavour to keep a margin in my book open, to add here and there a note in shorthand with my own hand.

'And so I betake myself to that course, which is almost as much as to see myself go into my grave; for which, and all the discomforts that will accompany my being blind, the good God prepare me.

'S. P.'

Epilogue

WHEN Sam left for The Hague with Elizabeth, it may be doubted whether he looked forward very much to kissing the Dutch girls any more soundly than he had nine years before, in May 1660. Then he had been young, ambitious, gay and a grass widower. Now he was old—for thirty-seven was more like forty-seven in the seventeenth century—embittered by political and commercial intrigue, depressed by the failure of his sight, and with a snappishly jealous, though still beloved, wife forever at his heels. Even if he had continued to write up his Diary, there would probably have been less French, Spanish, Latin and Greek in it, less about 'doing what he would' and 'having opportunity' to investigate thighs and bosoms. It is known that he still worked hard on this journey, finding out everything he could about the state of the Dutch Navy, its personnel and finances, to be reported to the Duke of York on his return. He did the same when he passed into France a few weeks later.

But however much he enjoyed himself on the continent, an even more terrible catastrophe than Elizabeth's discovery of his passion for Deb Willet struck him on 10th November, shortly after his restoration to his native land and its two turbulent worlds, high and low, both of which he knew so well.

On that day, at the house in Crutched Friars, Mrs. Pepys succumbed to a fever she had caught in France. She was only twenty-nine. It is certain that Samuel was prostrated with grief. Even at her most maddening, Elizabeth had never ceased to command his deep devotion, both spiritual and sensual, though his physical infidelities to her add up to a formidable total and would have been even more numerous if he had not been such a busy man in other directions. Neither did he ever marry again, as nine men out of ten in his position would have done in those days. In spite of constant rows and the awful final disaster of the Deb case, they had been happier together than most married couples with restless tempers in any age.

Mr. Pepys erected a stately monument to his wife's memory at St. Olave's church in Hart Street, a short distance from the house, with a long and elegant Latin inscription, which declared, among other tributes, that she was childless only because no future being could compare with her.

For some two years after the death of Mrs. Pepys nothing is known of the bereaved husband's doubtless half-stunned existence. In 1672, moreover, a fire broke out in the Navy Office residences and they were all burnt to the ground. Samuel lost almost all the property in his house except his books, which were, characteristically, his first thought, luckily for the preservation of the Diary.

This year too, on 28th May, Lord Sandwich, Pepys' ever benevolent patron and cousin, was drowned in the hour of his squadron's victory at the battle off Solebay in Suffolk during a third Dutch war. This conflict had not arisen on commercial grounds, as had the two previous campaigns, but as a result of the ambitions of Louis XIV; the Grand Monarque was after the Spanish territory in the Netherlands and had bribed Charles II to back him in a bid for them against the United Provinces and Sweden.

The Duke of York, in command of the combined English and French fleets, with Sandwich as his immediate subordinate, was surprised at anchor by de Ruyter just after sunrise. The earl, repeating his former daring tactics, at once hoisted sail, ran up his 'Follow me!' signal and stood in towards the enemy, his guns thundering. He routed the squadron opposed to him. The Dutch admiral leading it himself fell. But

Sandwich's own flagship caught fire, and he died, like Nelson, knowing that 'they ran'.

The French ships declined battle, and the triumphant de Ruyter gave James' depleted forces a terrible hammering; but the Dutchman did not pursue his advantage, and the engagement ended indecisively. Sandwich was the best admiral Charles ever had, and was easily the most attractive of the great men whom Samuel knew well, with Evelyn a good second and Coventry a fair third.

In the summer of 1673 Samuel was appointed Secretary of the Admiralty, newly so named, and went to live in Westminster. In the autumn he was elected to Parliament, accused of Catholicism—excitement over a 'Popish Plot', with Louis behind it, was then raging—but acquitted. During the next few years honours fell thick upon him. In 1676 he was made Master of Trinity House, the ancient corporation in charge of lighthouses and the care of naval veterans, and in the following year Master of the Clothworkers' Company. The silver cup he then presented to the Company is still used at its banquets.

At the election of 1679 he was again returned to Parliament, but soon afterwards sent to the Tower on the former trumped up charge of 'papacy', to which was now added that of betraying naval secrets to the French. The accusation was of course quite baseless. It was, on the contrary, the naval secrets of the French which Pepys had passed on to the Duke of York in 1669. The Secretary was soon released from the Tower, and was formally acquitted in February 1680.

In that year he wrote the second of his three published works, a narrative of Charles II's escape from the battle of Worcester in 1651, which he took down in shorthand from the King's own lips at Newmarket in October. Both Charles and his brother, the Duke of York, were fond of Mr. Pepys, though it was to the latter, so closely associated with the Navy, that Samuel gave his most undivided loyalty.

In 1683-4 Pepys was at Tangier in connection with the abandonment of this post by the British Government. On his return he was appointed President of the Royal Society, of which he had been a member for nearly twenty years. In the following year King Charles died and was succeeded by his brother as James II, so long Pepys' generous patron while Duke of York. But again Samuel was unlucky. The new king, so kind, energetic and able as Duke and Admiral, proved a wretched monarch, tactless and quarrelsome to a degree; he made no special effort to advance the fortunes of his former favourite.

But Mr. Pepys was still highly regarded by others, and he was again elected to Parliament in 1685. However, the 'Glorious Revolution' was at hand. James was exiled, and all those who had followed him in the past were dropped from office when his son-in-law, the Dutchman William of Orange, came to the British throne. The Secretary of the Admiralty laid down his office on 9th March 1689.

The inevitable persecution ensued. He was again accused of betraying naval secrets, and imprisoned for a short time in the summer of 1690. On his release, by now a definitely sick man, though he never seems to have gone really blind, agitation against him still continued.

He employed his enforced leisure in composing a volume of *Memoirs of the Navy* which was published before the end of the year, and also in correspondence with many friends and work as Treasurer of Christ's Hospital.

On 26th May 1703 John Evelyn, the other great contemporary Diarist, wrote in his journal: 'This day died Mr. Sam Pepys, a very worthy, industrious and curious person, none in England exceeding him in knowledge of the navy, in which he had passed through all the most considerable offices . . . all of which he performed with great integrity. When K. James II went out of England he laid down his office and would serve no more, but withdrawing himself from all public affaires he liv'd at Clapham with his partner Mr. Hewer, formerly his clerk, in a very noble and sweete place, where he enjoy'd the fruits of his labours in greate prosperity. He was universally belov'd, hospitable, generous, learned in many things, skill'd in music, a very greate cherisher of learned men of whom he had the conversation . . .'

Evelyn and Pepys were in fact close friends, and the latter always thought most highly of his 'ingenious' contemporary. But the two men were amusingly contrasted in their tastes and habits. Evelyn's domestic life was dignified and imperturbable. He was deeply pious and hated profligates, gossip, especially of the coarse and inquisitive kind, and every kind of low company. He really admired Pepys only as an administrator, though he could not have been insensitive to the Secretary's personal charm.

Administrators are not particularly popular characters today. The average modern citizen may occasionally respect them; he can never love them. But Sam Pepys would be welcome almost anywhere in 1958—except perhaps in that Whitehall he was so fond of, a very different place then.

Though really a bit of what Matthew Arnold used to call a Philistine, this stalwart official and indefatigable amorist had musical gifts of quite a high order, both as exponent and composer. He set at least four songs at the height of his business and erotic career; he played the lute, various forms of violin, the flute, the flageolet and the spinet; his ear was extremely sensitive and accurate. So much is proved by his frequent frenzied outbursts against bad playing and singing, as well as by his equally extravagant ecstasies over 'ravishing' performances. In short, he was genuinely never so happy, not even with the Pierces, Knipps, Lanes, Bagwells, Michells, Nells, Janes and the incomparable Deb herself, as when singing or playing in company.

As for books, they, with music, were one of the reasons why his sight failed him. As a moralist—for Pepys of the many kisses could be severe enough in other directions—he admired the practical good sense of Bacon. As a politician he deplored Hobbes, the defender of benevolent despotism. He did not read much theology, but he listened with keenly critical attention every Sunday to the oral delivery of sermons. They gave him nearly as many alternate fits of indignation and rapture as music inspired in him.

He did not really care for poetry except, characteristically, Chaucer's gossipy tales, or for satire. He read such literature only to be in the fashion. Nor, strangely enough, does he seem very interested in pornography. What he really loved was the drama. After the re-opening of the theatres closed by the Puritans in 1642 the whole age became stage-struck, but Sam outdid most of his contemporaries in his passionate addiction to every aspect of theatrical life, which came a very good second indeed to music and women—of course it always presented a certain quantity of both—in his relaxations. Many plays he saw over and over again with the greatest possible enjoyment. Others infuriated him.

He adored nearly all actresses, especially if they were 'merry'; but, with the possible exception of the good-natured Mary Knipp, he could not afford to make any of them his mistresses. He could only swallow the scandalous chatter about them, as eagerly as if it were about the Court, which, in part, it very often was—for every fashionable aristocrat of the day strained every nerve to give at least the impression that the playhouse stars twinkled for him alone.

Pepys was also fond of pictures. He spent many hours looking at prints and bought a few, but like most English amateurs he preferred portraits to landscape or still-life. Both he and his wife were painted by leading artists in London, notably Lely and Kneller. One of the many portraits of Lady Castlemaine graced his private office.

Yet in spite of all these aesthetic interests, to which we must add his connoisseurship of the female form, especially its hand, Samuel was more at home with bureaucrats, sailors and business men than with artists or writers, if we except John Evelyn, though he was careful what he said to that respectable gentleman. The tavern and the plutocratic drawing-room—the rowdier the better—were more in his line than intellectual society or the company of great nobles. Sam was no genius, talented as he was in many directions, including the difficult one of 'amours'. Nor did he ever pretend to be anyone out of the ordinary. His very real modesty is one of his most endearing traits. For the first twenty years of his career, at any rate, he remained secretly astounded at his rapid rise to glory.

As to his other virtues, a considerable streak of vulgarity did not prevent his being the most tender-hearted and loyal of friends. Moreover, he kept absolutely honest in the corrupt world of intrigue to which he was doomed as a seventeenth-century administrator. To this uncompromising sincerity, one of the rarest merits of human character, he added what so often goes with it, great courage and resolution—except where those minor 'good resolutions' were concerned, which he failed with such signal regularity to keep. He was said by his doctor to have died in really noble fashion.

He could be uncommonly foolish in his private life, alternately as vain and abject as old Jack Falstaff himself, but far too unsophisticated to laugh at himself in the Shakespearian manner. In fact, Sam must be one of the few cases on record of an utterly delightful man with no sense of humour whatever, though forever in search of 'mirth'. Part of the fascination of the Diary arises from its solemnity of style in relating absurd or morally discreditable incidents, especially such as are usually not considered worth discussing or proper to be discussed in polite society. These passages, written by a man whose own secret life was so highly questionable, make all the more impact for being quite innocent of any attempt at irony, deliberate obscenity or teasing or exciting the reader. It is probable that he never dreamed of having a reader at all.

In any case, he was quite incapable of consciously contrived literary effects. Fond though he was of books, he read them simply out of curiosity, not to appreciate methods of composition. His own writing is quite devoid of aesthetic distinction, polished phraseology and even decent grammar; yet it is incomparably vivid. One hears his very voice throughout, that warm, hesitant, slipshod speech so typical of ordinary English life then as now. For this reason the Diary is historically, if not artistically, priceless. Here, and here only, is King Charles's

London, brutal and gay, passionate and industrious, tough to the very bone and formidably independent of the anxious men, Pepys himself among them, who tried to rule it. No greater contrast could be imagined to the hypocritically genteel, nervously febrile, fundamentally supine and apathetic London society of today.

quiddity - that which distinguishes a thing from others, and makes it what it is. A captious question, a trifling question - destinction

albeit - even though, although

maladroit - badly

percheron - large fast trotting draft horse.

lustrum - a five year period.

japeries - joking

The last good japery I experienced was about 2 lustrum past, perched on a fast moving percheron